iMovie

Beginner's Guide

Complete Beginner to Expert Guide to Master the Latest
Tools, Techniques & Tips Stunning Video Production

Quentin Fox

Disclaimer and Terms of Use

The author and publisher of this book and the accompanying materials have used their best efforts in preparing this book. The author and publisher make no representation or warranties with respect to the accuracy, applicability, fitness, or completeness of the contents of this book. The information contained in this book is strictly for informational purposes. Therefore, if you wish to apply the ideas contained in this book, you are taking full responsibility for your actions.

Printed in the United States of America

TABLE OF CONTENTS

INTRODUCTION

Welcome to the exciting world of iMovie, where with just a few clicks you can make your dull videos look amazing. iMovie is your reliable video editing companion, whether you're a casual photographer who wants to record life's special moments or a hopeful director with big ideas. We are going to take a thrilling journey through the ins and outs of iMovie in this complete guide. We will find a great trove of tools and techniques that will change the way you tell stories through video. From the most basic things like cutting and sorting clips to the more complex things like adding effects and transitions, we'll talk about it all. No need to worry if you've never edited a movie before! We'll be here for you every step of the way, breaking down hard ideas into manageable chunks that even the most inexperienced novices can understand. With clear instructions and real-life examples, you'll quickly be able to use iMovie like a pro and make videos that amaze and please people. iMovie is more than just a piece of software, though. It's a way to show yourself and your talent in ways you never thought possible. As we learn more about its features, we'll see how it lets writers of all levels—from amateurs to seasoned pros—bring their ideas to life with great movie flair. Here we go! Prepare for an exciting journey through the world of iMovie, where every change is a brilliant idea and every shift a magical moment. If you have this guide with you, the options are endless. Let's dive in and learn more about the amazing world of making videos!

CHAPTER 1
ABOUT IMOVIE

Understanding iMovie

Apple Inc.'s iMovie stands out as flexible and easy-to-use software for changing videos that can be used by both new and experienced users. Making high-quality movies is easy with it, and there isn't a steep learning curve like there is with professional editing suites. The structure of the iMovie interface is made to be simple for users to use. Its workspace has important parts like a video viewing window, a timeline for organizing clips, and a toolbar with different editing tools. The software is easy to learn and use, so users can get started on their editing projects right away without feeling overwhelmed. One of the best things about iMovie is how well it works with Apple products. Videos can be easily imported from cameras, iPhones, iPads, and other cameras, as well as from external hard drives or other video editing tools. This integration makes editing easier by letting users access their media files without having to go through time-consuming import steps. A full set of editing tools is available in iMovie, which can be used for a wide range of tasks. iMovie has all the tools users need to make their videos look better in creative ways. It has basic tools like trimming, splitting, and merging clips, as well as more advanced tools like adding transitions, titles, and effects. In addition, iMovie has some styles and templates that users can easily use in their projects. These themes are already made and come with titles, transitions, and music. This means that users can get results that look professional without having to spend a lot of time or energy editing. Another place where iMovie shines is audio editing. To improve the sound quality of their movies, users can change the volume, add background music, change the audio tracks, and add audio effects. With this wide range of audio editing tools, users can make videos with immersive audio experiences that go well with the visual material.

iMovie also has a green screen tool that lets users change the background of their videos to a different picture or video clip. This feature enables users to take their subjects to any place or setting they can think of, which greatly enhances their creative potential. For users who want to share their work after editing, iMovie has many options. iMovie gives users the freedom to share their movies with the people they want to see them by letting them export the project directly to social media sites like YouTube and Vimeo, save it to their device, or burn it to a DVD to watch later. To sum up, learning how to use iMovie is necessary for anyone who wants to easily make high-quality movies. Its powerful editing tools, easy-to-use interface, seamless integration with Apple devices and wide range of sharing options make it essential tools for making artistic ideas come to life. People can reach their full potential as video makers and make content that engages and inspires their audience by getting to know iMovie's features and trying out different editing methods.

Get Around the Interface

There are three main places in iMovie, which you can usually find at the top of the screen unless you already have a project open:

- **Media**: This is where you keep your files; you may have various libraries that hold various types of media.
- **Projects** are a list of all the projects you've updated. If you're performing a different edit on a project, it can be helpful to copy it here. You will be asked to choose between a Movie and a Trailer project when you start a new project. Choose the Movie project.
- **Theater**: Here you can watch movies you've downloaded or shared, or you can make a new movie or trailer.

Most of the time, iMovie starts the last project you edited. Choose **File/New Movie** to make a project if you haven't already. After that, iMovie will take you to the project view for your new movie. iMovie is split into 3 separate places in this project view.

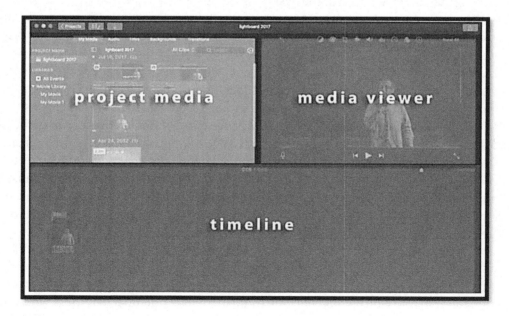

- **Project Media**. The media for your project is on the left side of your screen. There will be quick views of your iPhoto library, songs from your iTunes library and GarageBand, and any media that you may have imported into this. iMovie makes libraries for your media, which you can see here. This is also where you can find titles, backgrounds, and transitions.
- **Media Viewer**. It's possible to view the media in your stream or the media you've chosen in the project media area on the right. There is a lot of color and audio correction options above the media player, so you can change the colors, crop an image, give a media clip the Ken Burns effect, and do a lot of other useful editing.
- **Timeline**. You can edit video clips and change the audio in the timeline of your edited media at the bottom.

Organizing your media

If you don't, you might end up with media from multiple projects in your main iMovie Library. It can get pretty hard to sort through media from different projects for several years. The media in your iMovie library is divided into events, which are then organized by date. Quick tip for saving space on your screen: By unchecking "**Show Separated Days in Events**" in the View menu, you can hide the event names. When you look over video clips, you might find a good part of one of them. You can mark that part of the video as a favorite by pressing the F computer shortcut or going to **Mark > Favorite**. On the other hand, if you find a bad part of a clip, you can reject it by pressing the delete key on your keyboard or picking **Mark/Delete**. You can later sort your media so that you only see the clips you've liked. This can help when you have a lot of clips to look through.

Importing your media into iMovie

Media from anywhere on your computer can be dragged and dropped onto the timeline of your project. The media will then be saved to your iMovie project library.

Importing your media from the Photos app

You may have imported videos or photos into the Photos app. You can easily add these to your project by these steps:

- Click on **Photos Library** under **Libraries** in the **Project Media** area, and then select the **My Media** tab to import videos. You can choose your material in some ways. One way is to go to **Albums** and then **Videos**. Move the video to the timeline of your project.
- Select the **My Media** tab in the **Photos Library** to import photos. If you want to import photos, one way is to choose Years, then find the photos you want to use and drag them onto the timeline of your project.

Customization Options

The many customization options in iMovie let users make their videos better by adding creative effects, transitions, titles, and audio changes.

Here are some of the most important ways that iMovie can be customized:

- **Themes**: iMovie has many themes that give your videos a style that's already been thought out. To give your video a unified appearance, themes include matching titles, transitions, and effects.
- **Transitions**: iMovie lets you choose from some transitions that make switching between clips smooth. You can dissolve, slide, wipe, and do other things using these options. For accurate timing, you can also change how long transitions last.
- **Filters**: You can use filters to change the mood or look of your video. iMovie has some filters that can be easily applied to clips or the whole video.
- **Titles**: iMovie has built-in title tools that you can use to give your video titles and credits that look professional. To make your titles stand out, you can change the text, style, size, color, and animation effects.
- **Effects**: Add effects like slow motion, fast forward, quick replay, picture-in-picture, green screen, and more to your clips to make them better. These effects can help you be more creative and tell stories in your movies.
- **Audio**: iMovie lets you change the volume of the audio, add background music, add sound effects, and record voiceovers right in the program. To enhance the sound quality, you can also use audio effects such as normalization and noise reduction.
- **Speed Control**: To make dramatic or funny effects, you can change the speed of your clips. It's easy to speed up or slow down video in iMovie.
- **Color Correction**: Use iMovie's color correction tools to make small changes to your video's colors and brightness. To get the look you want, change the white balance, brightness, contrast, and color.
- **Green Screen**: The green screen feature in iMovie lets you make interesting visual effects. You can use this to change the background of a clip to a different picture or video.
- **Sharing Options**: iMovie gives you some sharing options after you've edited your video. You can save your video to your computer, share it directly on social media sites, or export it to a different resolution.

Project Settings and Preferences

1. **Project Settings:**
   - **Resolution:** iMovie allows you to choose the resolution of your project, including options like 720p, 1080p, and 4K. Selecting the appropriate resolution depends on your intended output and the quality you desire.

- **Aspect Ratio:** You can set the aspect ratio of your project to standard options such as 16:9 (widescreen) or 4:3 (standard). This setting determines the shape and dimensions of your video.
- **Frame Rate:** Choose the frame rate for your project, typically ranging from 24 to 60 frames per second (fps). Higher frame rates result in smoother motion but may require more processing power.
- **Theme:** iMovie offers various themes that provide pre-designed styles for your project. Themes include matching titles, transitions, and effects that enhance the overall look of your video.
- **Audio Settings:** Adjust audio settings such as sample rate and audio format (AAC or uncompressed) based on your preferences and the quality you require for your project's sound.

2. **Preferences:**
   - **General Preferences:** Customize general settings such as the default project location, automatic video cropping, and keyboard shortcuts. You can also choose whether to show advanced tools in the toolbar.
   - **Import Preferences:** Configure settings related to importing media, such as how clips are organized (by date or keyword), whether to copy files into the library, and options for optimizing video and audio during import.
   - **Playback Preferences:** Adjust playback settings, including the default volume level, the behavior of the playhead during playback, and options for audio monitoring while recording voice overs.
   - **Sharing Preferences:** Customize settings for sharing your projects, such as the resolution and quality of exported videos, social media accounts for sharing directly from iMovie, and options for including metadata in shared files.
   - **Timeline Preferences:** Fine-tune settings related to the timeline, such as clip duration when dragging to the timeline, snapping behavior, audio waveforms display, and background rendering preferences.
   - **Library Preferences:** Manage settings for your iMovie library, including storage optimization, automatic deletion of projects and events, and options for backing up your library to external drives or iCloud.

CHAPTER 2
GETTING STARTED WITH IMOVIE

Installation Procedures

1. **Mac Computer:**
   - Open the App Store on your Mac.
   - Search for "iMovie" in the search bar.
   - Once you locate iMovie in the search results, click on the "Get" or "Download" button.
   - Follow the on-screen instructions to complete the installation process.
   - After installation, iMovie should appear in your Applications folder, and you can launch it from there.

2. **iPhone or iPad:**
   - Open the App Store on your iPhone or iPad.
   - In the search bar, type "iMovie" and press enter.
   - Find iMovie in the search results and tap on it.
   - Tap the "Get" button next to iMovie to download and install it on your device.
   - Once the installation is complete, you can find iMovie on your home screen and launch it to start editing videos.

3. **iCloud (For Automatic Installation on Multiple Devices):**
   - If you have multiple Apple devices linked to the same iCloud account, you can enable automatic downloads for iMovie.
   - On your Mac, go to the Apple menu > System Preferences > iCloud.
   - Make sure the "Apps" option is checked under iCloud Drive.
   - On your iPhone or iPad, go to Settings > [your name] > iCloud.
   - Enable iCloud Drive and ensure that the "iMovie" toggle is turned on.
   - This setup allows iMovie to automatically download and install on all your Apple devices linked to the same iCloud account.

4. **App Store on Apple TV:**
   - If you want to install iMovie on your Apple TV, open the App Store on your Apple TV device.
   - Navigate to the search bar and type "iMovie."
   - Select iMovie from the search results and click on the "Download" button to install it on your Apple TV.

After following these installation steps, you should have iMovie successfully installed and ready to use on your Apple device. Keep in mind that iMovie may come pre-installed, so you might not need to download it separately in those cases.

Creating a New Project

1. Click the "+" button in the Projects gallery. To get to the Projects browser while you're still changing a movie, press Done and then Projects.
2. Click on Movie. All the video clips and pictures from a specific day or event are displayed on the Moments screen, which is a collection of media from your pictures app photo library.
    a. To make a trailer with your movies and photos, you can also tap **Trailer** and use one of the built-in templates.
3. To view pictures or video clips in a bigger size, tap and hold the thumbnail.
4. Either tap a photo or video clip that you want to add to your movie, or tap Select to pick a full scene. Items that are chosen have a tick next to them. Go to step 6 if you don't want to add media from your photo library.
5. Tap **Media**, then tap another folder to view more video clips, pictures, and files.
6. Press "**Create Movie**." The new project starts. The timeline shows the videos or pictures you chose. The timeline is empty if you didn't add any pictures or videos.

You can always add pictures and videos to your project after you've already made the movie. When you use iMovie on your iPhone or iPad, the size of your movie is set by the best clip in your project. To give you an idea, if you add a 4K video clip to your project, you can share it at 4K resolution.

Record directly into iMovie

You can add a video or picture straight from your iPhone or iPad's camera to your iMovie project:

1. Open your project in iMovie and move the playhead (the white line that looks like a cross) to where you want to add the video or picture.

2. Press and hold the "+" button on your iPhone, then press and hold the "Camera"  button. Press the **Camera button** on your iPad.

3. Use the camera's controls to set options like flash and resolution before tapping the Record button ⬤.

4. When you're done recording a video, press the "**Stop**" button. Go to the next step if you took a picture.

5. Press "**Use Video**" or "**Use Photo**" to add the video or photo to the project list. You can also press "Retake" to take the picture or video again.

When you open the iMovie timeline, the new clip is where the playhead was.

How to create a new iMovie project on your Mac

1. Click "**Create New**" in the Projects window. Once you're done changing a movie, go to the toolbar and click the Projects button. This will open the Projects browser.

2. Click on **Movie**. The browser, viewer, and timeline appear when your new project starts.

If you click on Trailer, you can use the built-in templates to make your trailer with your photos and movies.

3. Once you've made your project, add clips from events from the Libraries list or photos and video clips from your Photos app library. **You can also import media such as photos, video clips, and other media from outside sources:**

   - Import from iPhone or iPad
   - Import from cameras that record to flash drives or another file-based storage system
   - Import media from your Mac
   - Record video directly into iMovie using your Mac

Click on the iMovie window and drag clips to the timeline of your project to begin making your movie. You can also drag clips into the timeline from your Mac's Finder or Desktop.

Importing Media Files

Import into iMovie on Mac from iPhone or iPad

1. Connect Your Device: Start by using the USB cord that came with your iOS device to connect it to your Mac. Make sure that your Mac can see and connect to your gadget.

2. Open iMovie and go to the Import Window: Start up the iMovie app on your Mac. To get to the Import window, click on the Import button in the menu once the program is open.

You can click on the Media button in the toolbar first and then click on the Import button from that menu.

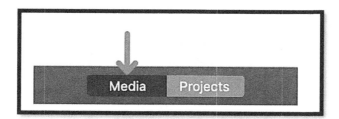

3. Choose Your Device: There is a sidebar with different parts in the Import window. Find the Cameras area in the sidebar and pick out your iOS device. This will get video clips and pictures on your device and show thumbnails of them in the Import window.

4. Preview and Select Media: While moving your mouse left and right over a video frame, you can see previews of video clips. You can also move the mouse over the preview area at the top of the Import window and press the Play button to see the sample. The Previous and Next buttons let you move between clips or go back or forward in a clip.

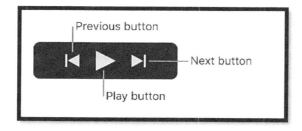

5. **Choose Where to Import**: There are two options for where the imported media will be kept:
- **Choose an existing event**: Select an existing event where you want to import the media by using the "Import to" pop-up button at the top of the Import window.

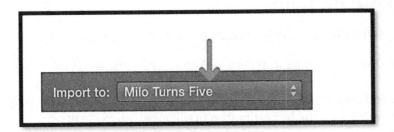

- **Create a new event**: If you'd rather make a new event, choose "**New Event**" from the "**Import to**" menu, give it a name, and click "**OK.**"

6. Import Media: Once you've chosen where to import the media, you can start the process:
- **Import All Clips**: Click "Import All" to import all of your device's videos.
- **Import selected clips**: Press command-click on each one you want to bring in and then click on "Import Selected." The Import button will change its name to reflect this.

7. **Keep an eye on the progress of the import**: In the upper right area of the window, you may see a progress bar while the media is being imported. While the import is going on, you can keep working in iMovie.

8. **Disconnect Your Device**: After the import is finished, you can disconnect your iOS device from your Mac, and the imported clips will show up in the appropriate event in iMovie.

Import into iMovie on Mac from file-based cameras

A camera or other device that works with files can record and save video clips and pictures on flash drives or hard disk drives (HDDs). Most file-based cameras and other gadgets use a USB cable to connect to your computer. You can use portable memory cards that come with some file-based cameras to connect them to your Mac instead. You can check the iMovie Supported Cameras page to see if your camera works with **iMovie... Import media** from your device into **iMovie on your Mac by performing the following steps.**

1. **Connect Your Device:**
- Use the cable provided with your device to connect it to your Mac.

- For camcorders, set them to PC Connect mode (the name of this mode may vary). Refer to your device's documentation for more information.
- **Note:** Connecting a DVD camcorder might open the DVD Player app. simply quit the DVD Player if this happens.

2. **Using an SD Card:**
   - If your device uses an SD card, eject it and insert it into your Mac's card slot (if available) or use an external card reader.

3. **Open iMovie and Access Import:**
   - Launch the iMovie app on your Mac.
   - Click the Import button in the toolbar to open the Import window. If you don't see the Import button, click the Media button first and then select Import.

4. **Select Your Device:**
   - In the Import window, navigate to the Cameras section in the sidebar and select your device. Thumbnails of video clips and photos from your device will appear in the Import window.

5. **Preview and Select Media:**
   - You can preview video clips by hovering your pointer over a thumbnail or using the playback controls.
   - Use the Previous and Next buttons to navigate between clips or to rewind/fast-forward within a clip.

6. **Specify Import Location:**
   - Choose where the imported media will be stored:
     - Select an existing event from the "Import to" pop-up menu at the top of the Import window.
     - Or create a new event by choosing "New Event" from the pop-up menu, entering a name, and clicking OK.

7. **Import Media:**
   - Import all clips by clicking Import All or select specific clips by Command-clicking each and then clicking Import Selected.

8. **Monitor Import Progress:**
   - A progress indicator may appear in the upper-right corner of the window while importing.
   - You can continue working in iMovie during the import process.

9. **Disconnect Your Device:**
   - Once the import is complete, disconnect your device from your Mac.

Supported Media Formats

1. **Video Formats:**
   - MPEG-4 (MP4, MOV, and M4V): iMovie supports these popular video formats commonly used for recording and sharing videos.
   - QuickTime Movie (MOV): QuickTime MOV files are fully compatible with iMovie and maintain high-quality video.

- AVCHD (MTS, M2TS): Advanced Video Coding High Definition (AVCHD) format is commonly used in camcorders and is supported by iMovie.
- **DV and HDV:** Digital Video (DV) and High Definition Video (HDV) formats are supported for importing footage from camcorders.
- **Apple Animation Codec:** This codec is used for animated content and is compatible with iMovie.

2. **Audio Formats:**
- AAC (Advanced Audio Coding): AAC is a standard audio format used for high-quality audio compression and is supported by iMovie.
- MP3: iMovie can import MP3 audio files for use in video projects.
- WAV (Waveform Audio): WAV files containing uncompressed audio are compatible with iMovie.
- AIFF (Audio Interchange File Format): AIFF is another uncompressed audio format supported by iMovie.
- Apple Lossless: This format preserves audio quality while reducing file size and is compatible with iMovie.

3. **Image Formats:**
- JPEG (JPG): JPEG images are widely used and can be imported into iMovie for creating slideshows or incorporating images into videos.
- PNG (Portable Network Graphics): PNG images with transparent backgrounds are supported in iMovie for overlaying graphics.
- TIFF (Tagged Image File Format): TIFF images can be imported into iMovie for use in projects.

4. **Additional Formats:**
- H.264: iMovie can work with videos encoded using the H.264 codec, which is commonly used for web streaming and digital media.
- HEVC (H.265): High-Efficiency Video Coding (HEVC) is supported in iMovie for editing videos with efficient compression.
- ProRes: Apple ProRes video files are compatible with iMovie, providing high-quality editing options.

CHAPTER 3

ORGANIZE MEDIA AND EVENTS IN IMOVIE

If you choose to import video footage into your library, iMovie will organize the clips into events based on the date and time the video was taken. Your clips are stored in events, which are like folders. Even though events are initially grouped by time, you can group clips in any way you want. If you choose an event from the Libraries list, the clips that go with it will show up in the browser.

Click the Libraries List button at the top of the window if the list of libraries isn't there.

The Libraries list can be changed so that events are shown in any order you want.

Do any of these things in the iMovie app on your Mac:

- *Sort events by name*: Pick View > Sort Events By > Name.
- *Sort events from newest to oldest*: In View, go to Sort Events By and choose "Newest to Oldest."

When you sort events by date, events in each library are put together by year.

- *Sort events from oldest to newest*: In View, go to Sort Events By and select Oldest to Newest.

Create and Rename Events

1. Open the iMovie app on your Mac and choose the library where you want to add an event from the list of libraries.
2. Go to File > New Event.
   - The name of the new event is marked when it shows up in the Libraries list.
3. Type a new name for the event to change its name.

If you want to change the name of an existing event, pick it in the Libraries list, press Return, and type the new name.

Copy or move clips between events

1. In the Mac's iMovie app, go to the Libraries list and choose an event that has clips you want to move or copy.
2. Pick out the clips you want to move or copy in the browser.
Tip: Hold down the Command key and click on the clips you want to pick. You can also drag a selection rectangle around the clips to select them all at once.
3. Pick one of these things to do:
  - ***Move clips between events***: Drag the clips you've chosen from one event to the next.
  - ***Copy clips between events***: If you want to move the clips you've chosen from one event to another, hold down the Option key and start dragging.

If you select your project in the sidebar and then drag clips from the browser to the target event, the clips will be copied there.

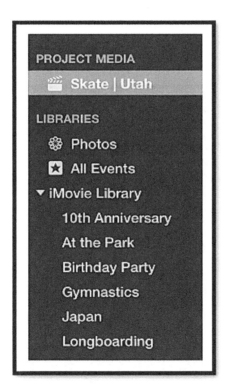

Duplicate Clips

  1. You can make a copy of a clip to try out different effects or changes without changing the original.

Choose the event in the Libraries list of the iMovie app on your Mac that has the clip you want to copy.

2. Select the clip you want to copy and double-click it.

If you pick out a piece of a clip, the whole thing will be copied.

Tip: Hold down the Command key and click on the clips you want to pick. You can also drag a selection rectangle around the clips to select them all at once.

3. Go to **Edit > Duplicate Movie.**

Merge or Split Events

If two or more events in the Libraries list have footage that is very closely linked, you can merge them. A single event can also be split into several events.

Do any of these things in the iMovie app on your Mac:

Merge events: Choose an event from the Libraries list and drag it to the event you want to merge with. You can also choose the events you want to merge and go to **File > Merge Events**.

- **Split a single event:** Create the new events you need, and then move clips from the original event to the new events.

Delete Clips and Events

You can get rid of clips from an event that you don't want and cancel the event itself to make room for other things.

Note: You have to delete a full event to make room for new events. When you delete clips from an event, the storage area doesn't get bigger.

1. Do one of these things in the iMovie app on your Mac:
   - To delete an event, go to the Libraries list and choose the event you want to get rid of.
   - ***Delete clips in an event***: To delete clips, first find the event you want to delete them from in the Libraries list. Then, in the browser, pick the clips you want to delete.

To choose more than one clip in the same library, hold down the Command key and click on the clips you want to choose. You can also drag a selection box around the clips to choose them all.

2. Go to **File > Move to Trash**.

If the file you want to delete is currently being used in a project, you will see a message telling you to remove it from the project first.

Note: If you choose a clip and press "Delete," it will be marked as "rejected."

Manage media imported to iMovie on iPad

In the iMovie Media part of the media browser, you can edit media used in projects that have been shared between devices. After that, you can either download the media to your Photos library or get rid of it from the device.

Note: This is also how you can handle media from projects you made in older versions of iMovie.

1. Open the iMovie app on your iPad and tap on a project in the **Projects tab**. Then, tap **Edit**.
2. Click on **Video**.
   - **Note**: If you can't see the media browser, click the "Add Media" button in the top right corner and then click "Video."
3. Click on **iMovie Media**.
   - Any video clips not already saved in your Photos library will show up here.
4. Click on **Edit**.
   - Each clip has a button on the right side of it.
5. Do one of these things:

   - *Save a clip to your Photos library*: Use the dark Download button to get it.
   - *Remove a clip from your device*: Press the red "Delete" button.
Please keep this in mind: If the clip is being used in a project, you need to remove it from the timeline first.

CHAPTER 4
BASIC EDITING TECHNIQUES
Trim Video in iMovie on iPhone/iPad

- **Step 1.** Open the iMovie app on your iPhone/iPad.
- **Step 2.** Create a new project by hitting the Movie option.

- **Step 3:** Pick the video from your album that you want to cut and add it to iMovie.

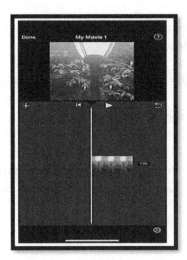

- **Step 4:** To see the timeline, touch the thumbnail of the video in the middle of the screen.
- **Step 5:** Move the sliders on both sides of the timeline to choose the parts of the video you want to keep. When you're done, click "Done."

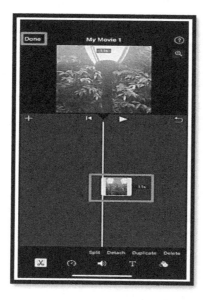

- **Step 6:** You can now watch a preview of the new video and choose whether to keep changing or save it.

Cut Videos in iMovie on Mac

Step 1. Startup **iMovie** on your Mac. Drag and drop the video you want to edit into the edit box by selecting **File > Import Media** or by using the drag-and-drop method.

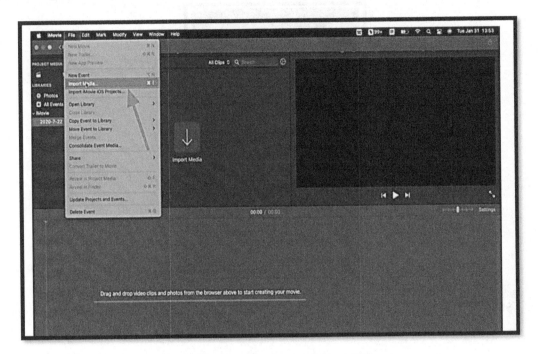

Step 2. Then, the video's timeline will appear on the editing screen. To cut or split the video, you can move the white vertical line to the exact spot you want.

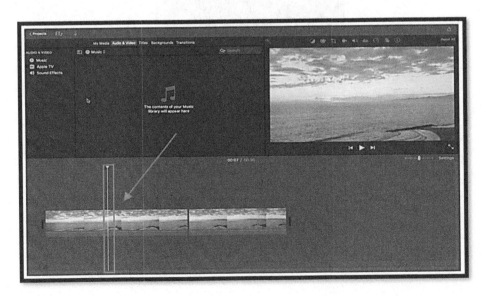

Step 3: Once you know where to cut the video, press the Command+B keys to split it in half.

Step 4: Press the Delete key to get rid of the part you don't want to keep.
Step 5: Now press the Spacebar to see a sneak peek of the new video. You can save it on your Mac or share it on some sites.

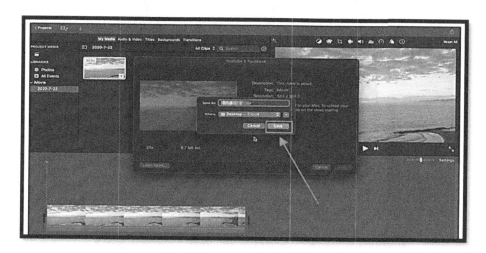

Splitting Techniques

Splitting Clips on Mac

Using iMovie to split a video is an easy process. To learn how to split a video clip on a Mac, follow these steps:

- **Step 1:** Drag the project or video you want to work on into the timeline in iMovie to open it.

- **Step 2:** Use your mouse to move the playhead to the first frame of the new scene and place it by clicking once.
- **Step 3:** In the main menu bar, you will find the "**Modify**" option. Pick the "**Split Click**" option. To split the original video into two separate clips, you can also press Command + B on the keyboard.

Splitting Clips on iPhone or iPad

To edit a project, tap its name. The "Projects" page will open the details of the video or movie project you want to edit. Click **Edit**. You can find this button below the title and image of the video. The chosen video will be opened in the editor. Drag the video roll at the bottom while holding it down. On your screen, you can find the video roll. Hold it down and drag it to the exact spot where you want to split the video.

- The bottom part of the screen will show you a roll of the whole video that you can edit.
- Place the white, vertical playhead on the exact point in the clip where you want to split it.

To choose the clip, tap it. This will make the clip stand out in the editor with a yellow outline, and the editing tools will appear at the bottom of the screen.

- If you pinch outward, you can get a better view of the clip and pick a better split point.

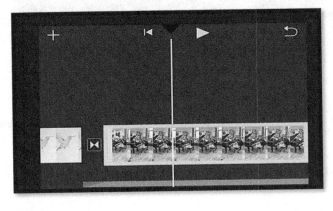

Pick out the scissors icon. The Actions icon may already be chosen when you choose a movie by default. It looks like knives and is far to the left. It will show you a list of editing options, one of which is Split.

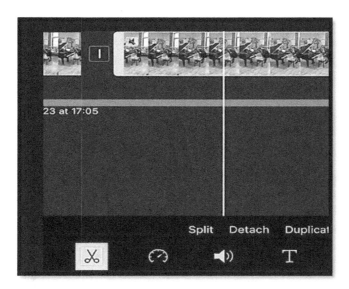

Click on Split, which is above the bottom menu. The video will be cut off where the white vertical line is.

- **Following the split, you will have two clips to edit separately.**
    - One way to do this is to split a clip in half along the edges of some frames you want to remove. Then, tap the new part and select "Delete" from the menu that appears.

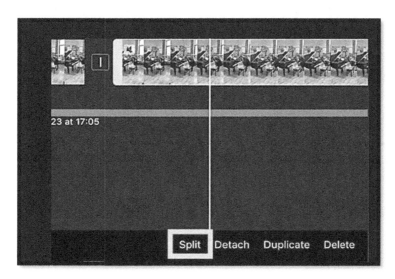

Speed Up and Slow Down Video

- Open the interface; select the File option, then select Import Media to add the file you want to edit to the main interface.
- The panel for changing the video will appear when you double-click on the video clip. You can edit the numbers in the speed panel to specify how quickly or slowly you want the video clip to play by selecting the Speed option. You can watch the video in the preview window to find the best speed effect for it.

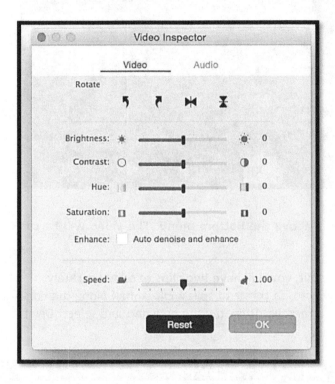

- You can export the video clip with the new speed settings in a different file type once you're happy with the effect. You can put this on YouTube or make a new DVD from the file inside.

How to speed up and slowdown in iMovie

- Go to **File > Options** and click on New Event. You can write down the event's speed.
- Choose the movie file you want to edit by clicking on the **Import Media** option.
- Move the Playhead to the spot in the video where you want the clip to go. To divide the entire timeline into two different parts, right-click on this point and select the Split Clip option.
- There are many places on the clip where you can split it, in the same way, to add speed-up and slow-down effects.

- Now pick a split clip and click on the **Seed button**, which is right above the main viewer. From the pull-down menu, you can change the speed to fast or slow, whichever you like.
- To change how the clip looks, click on the presets for speed and try out different speed options.

How to Use the Precision Editor

The Precision Editor shows everything about a transition that isn't shown on the timeline. It can be scary to use the Precision Editor at first because it changes the style of the timeline, but it's a very useful tool once you get used to it.

You can use it successfully in this way:

- When you click on a transition icon on the timeline, two arrows show up below it.
- Press and hold the two button keys to open the Precision Editor.
- Use two fingers to poke out the timeline and zoom in on it to get a better look at the Precision Editor.
- **Click on the question mark to bring up the Help menu. The tooltips in this menu can help you understand the Precision Editor's many handles and other features:**

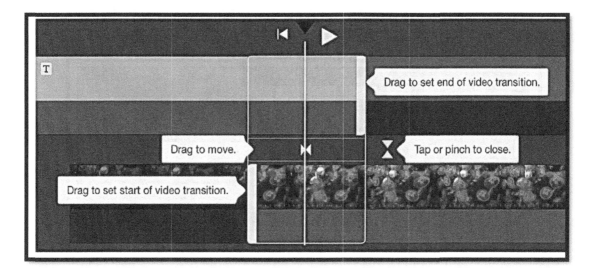

Now, let's take a look at what the Precision Editor can do since you can change a lot of different parts:

- The space that the transition takes up is shown by a thin yellow line. To move the whole transition left or right, hold down and drag the middle mark, which looks like two triangles facing each other:
  - Moving the transition to the left makes both clips begin earlier.
  - When you move the transition to the right, both clips start later.

- Parts of the video strip for the clip are darker and grayed out. These parts show the clip's parts that aren't being used. These lines go on forever for a picture because images don't have a set length.
- You can fine-tune the transition with separate handles. As you drag one of the thick yellow handles, it will change where the transition is on only one of the clips.

Then why would you want to use the Precision Editor? One reason is that it's the simplest way to move a whole transition to a different time. To do this in the timeline, you have to change the trim handles for both clips before and after the transition many times. You can also use different parts of video clips without cutting them in half by moving the transition button but not the handles. You can also work with sound very well in the Precision Editor. If you use a cross-dissolve or another long transition, the sounds from both clips will play at the same time, fighting with each other and making a lot of noise.

You can stay away from this in a few ways:

1. To move the transition to the right, drag the transition icon or one of the yellow handles. If you can't move the whole transition, move one of the handles. As the time difference between the two clips grows, this will make it less likely that sounds will clash.
2. If the transition has sound, you can use the thick blue handle to cut or add to the audio where it starts and stops. If you drag both blue handles so they're in the same vertical position, one will play audio where the other stops and the sounds won't clash:

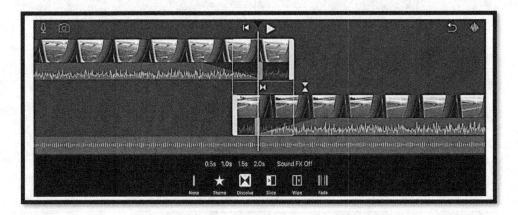

3. Arrow icons pointing in from the end of each clip indicate that the audio has been edited within the transition when you tap on the timeline to leave the Precision Editor.

Now that you know how to closely edit audio, let's talk about how to make the audio in your project better in general.

Fine-tuning Edits

Editing photos in Movie mode

From the **Start New Project** bar at the bottom of the Projects screen, choose **Movie**. In the Movie mode timeline, pictures and videos are handled in very different ways. There are fewer editing options, and you can't do as many things with photos on the timeline. You can only put the playhead at the beginning or end of a picture. If you tap on a photo, it will move to the left or right edge of the clip. This is why you can't split shots in Movie mode; you can only cut them off at the ends. Also, photos don't work the same way in the Viewer as most movies do. This is because of how they are shaped and how they fit in the video frame.

Using photo animations – the Ken Burns effect

Sometimes, iMovie won't show the whole picture when you add it to the timeline. This can happen if you use an iPad or take a portrait photo. The picture and video don't have the same aspect ratio, so this is what you see. The ratio of a frame's length to its height is called its aspect ratio. If this ratio is different from the Viewer's aspect ratio, the picture won't fill the whole screen. The picture will either be too tall or too wide to fit in the frame all the way. Most pictures are too tall. This is fixed by iMovie by zooming in on the picture so that it fills the whole screen. This is called "**crop to fill**." A tiny part of the picture fills the whole frame when the **crop to fill** is turned on. Then, iMovie automatically adds a motion to the picture, making it move across or up and down so you can see as much of it as possible. The Ken Burns effect is the name of the animation style you will have seen in **Magic Movie**. You can change or disable Ken Burns's cartoons in Movie mode, but you cannot edit them in Magic Movie.

That's easy to do:

1. Click on a picture in the timeline. The effect controls will appear in the bottom left area.

2. The option or menu that is currently chosen in iMovie is shown in blue. There is an option in the Viewer called "Pinch to position the start." It will also be clear from where the playhead is placed whether you are changing the animation's beginning or ending.

3. If you pinch the Viewer at the beginning of the clip, the animation will begin at a different place. **Here's what you can do:**

- To zoom in, spread your fingers apart.
- Pinch two fingers together to make the image bigger.
- Use one finger to drag the frame to move it.

4. When you move the frame and see black around the sides, you've reached the edge of the picture. The picture will be bounced back by iMovie so that the whole frame is filled.

5. Once you're happy with where the animation starts, tap the second skip button (the triangle and vertical line). This will let you choose where it ends. If you **pinch to position the end**, it will turn blue to show that it is chosen.

6. Once you're happy with where the beginning and end of the video are, move the playhead back to the beginning of the video and press the play button at the top of the timeline. The frame should move smoothly between the start and end points you set in the Viewer.

7. You can turn off the Ken Burns effect if you don't like it on your video by tapping on the low-level option that says "**Ken Burns Enabled**." The Viewer will show that Ken Burns is turned off.

If you do turn off Ken Burns, the picture will still be cut off to fit the screen, which is not good. Putting the picture on top of something else will let you see the whole thing. When you "overlay" a clip, you put it on top of another clip in the project so it shows up higher on the timeline.

After that, the picture will be shown with a black edge around it. Don't rush if you want to change how layers look. Also, keep in mind that you can't choose where the video starts or ends when you use the Ken Burns effect. Only when the clip is over will the animation stop moving. It will begin immediately. In other words, you can't make the picture stay still for one second and then start an animation. If you can do that, movements will look a lot more natural and less strange.

CHAPTER 5
ADDING TRANSITIONS AND EFFECTS

Exploring Transitions

1. **Accessing Transitions:**
   - To access the transition options in iMovie, first, open your project in iMovie on your Mac.
   - Click on the "Transitions" button located in the toolbar above the timeline. This button typically looks like two overlapping squares or arrows indicating a transition.

2. **Types of Transitions:**
   - **Standard Transitions:** iMovie offers a range of standard transitions such as dissolve, fade, slide, wipe, and more. These transitions are suitable for most video projects and can be applied between clips to create smooth transitions.
   - **Theme-Specific Transitions:** If you're using a theme in your project, iMovie provides theme-specific transitions that match the style and mood of the theme. For example, a cinematic theme might include dramatic transitions, while a fun theme might offer playful transitions.
   - **Custom Transitions:** iMovie also allows you to create custom transitions by adjusting the duration, direction, and style of the transition between clips. This gives you greater flexibility and control over the transition effects in your video.

3. **Applying Transitions:**
   - Once you've selected the desired transition, simply drag it from the Transitions browser onto the timeline between two clips where you want the transition to occur.
   - You can adjust the duration of the transition by clicking on it in the timeline and dragging its edges to shorten or lengthen the transition period.

4. **Previewing Transitions:**
   - To preview how a transition looks in your video, use the playback controls in iMovie to play the video from the timeline.
   - You can also use the spacebar on your keyboard to play and pause the video and observe how the transition blends between the clips.

5. **Fine-Tuning Transitions:**
   - iMovie allows you to fine-tune transitions by adjusting the transition type, duration, and additional settings.
   - Double-clicking on a transition in the timeline opens the Transition Adjustments window, where you can customize the transition properties, such as speed, direction, and style.

6. **Cross-Dissolve Transition:**
   - The cross-dissolve transition is a commonly used transition that gradually fades from one clip into the next. It creates a smooth transition between scenes and is ideal for maintaining continuity in your video.
7. **Experimenting and Creativity:**
   - Don't be afraid to experiment with different transitions and combinations to find the ones that best suit your video's style and narrative.
   - Use transitions sparingly and strategically to avoid overwhelming the viewer with too many effects.

Steps for adding transition effects to videos on iMovie

To "make a project," tap the plus sign.

- In the pop-up menu, tap on the movie option.

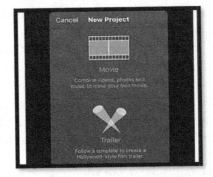

- Tap "**create movie**" and then choose the video you want to use as a transition in iMovie.
- To see the options, tap on the video below the timeline.

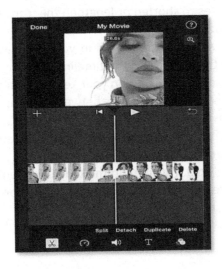

- Click on the "**split**" button next to the clip that you want to use the transition effect.

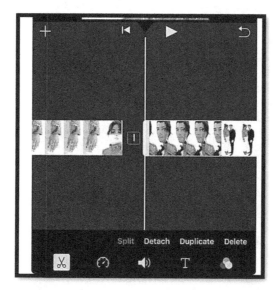

If you tap on the white line between the split clips, iMovie's transition options will appear.

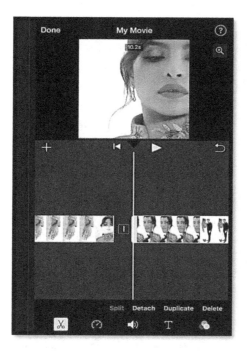

- Pick the kind of transition effect you want. iMovie has options for transitions like **fade, slide, wipe, dissolve, and theme.**

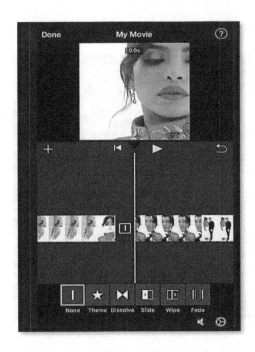

- Use the time limit option below to choose how long the transition effect will last.

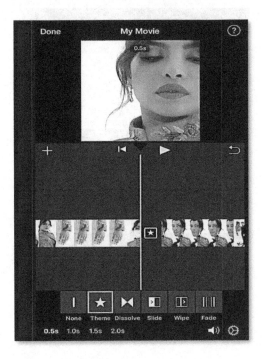

- To save your video, select the "done" option.
- To save your video to Photos, tap the arrow below.

How to add effects in iMovie

You can follow the numbered steps below to make use of video effects with iMovie:

- After starting the app, click **File > Import** to begin importing the video file or files you wants to work with. Users of iMovie can import MPEG, DV, and HDV video files.
- After importing the videos, go to the **Project Library** and click on a clip that you want to add effects to in iMovie. There will be a gear icon that you can use to click on **Clip Adjustments**. After that, an Inspector box will show up, and Video Effect: None will be in it.
- The library of free iMovie effects and filter options can be accessed by clicking on the Video Effect button. In iMovie, you can move your mouse over the effects to learn more about them and see what they do. Then, click on an effect you want to use to add it to your video.
- After adding the new effect, you'll be taken back to iMovie's main screen. In the top right corner, you can see what the effect will look like. Then, if you want, you can download more iMovie filters and add them to your file. If you're happy with the result, you can just save and export the file.

iMovie effects

There are different effects available for use in iMovie, including the following:

- **Color Adjustments**: Dive into the world of color manipulation! iMovie grants users the power to tweak and enrich the hues within each clip, transforming ordinary visuals into stunning spectacles.

- **Crop**: Say goodbye to unwanted distractions! With iMovie's cropping feature, you can tailor your clips to perfection, adjusting their dimensions and eliminating any pesky elements that detract from your masterpiece.
- **Rotation**: iMovie offers the flexibility to rotate clips to your heart's content, allowing for dynamic perspectives and unique compositions.
- **Stabilize**: iMovie's stabilization feature works wonders on shaky footage, ensuring a crystal-clear viewing experience that captivates your audience from start to finish.
- **Transitions**: Explore iMovie's extensive library of transitions, from elegant fades to eye-catching effects, effortlessly guiding viewers through your narrative journey.
- **Speed**: Adjust the tempo of your clips with iMovie's speed controls, whether you're slowing down for dramatic effect or revving up the pace for a thrilling sequence.
- **Filters**: iMovie offers a diverse array of filters to suit every style and mood, from timeless black and white to nostalgic retro vibes.
- **Green Screen**: iMovie's green screen effect empowers users to effortlessly remove backgrounds and transport subjects to new and exciting environments.
- **Split-Screen**: Double the impact with split-screen magic! iMovie lets you showcase multiple clips side by side, amplifying the drama and intrigue with dynamic juxtapositions.
- **Picture-in-Picture**: Enhance your storytelling with layered visuals! iMovie's picture-in-picture feature allows you to seamlessly integrate two images, enriching your narrative with compelling visual overlays.
- **Audio**: Fine-tune your soundscapes for maximum impact! With iMovie's audio effects, you can elevate your audio quality and layer multiple tracks to create immersive soundscapes that captivate and inspire.

Top 10 Effects in iMovie

Then, what are iMovie's top 10 effects? There are a lot of free effects for iMovie, but some are better than others. Here are our picks for the best effects for video editors:

1. Green/Blue Screen
For video producers on a tight budget, green and blue screens make life much simpler and less expensive. It's possible to record movies in front of a blue or green screen and then edit them in iMovie with any background you want. You can also remove a single color from the background or make that color see-through in your video. This lets you do a lot of cool visual effects.

2. Steadicam
You can get rid of shakes, wobbles, and movements in a video clip with a steadicam. People who make videos and shoot a lot of hand-held clips should use stabilization to make their videos look better and more professional. You can edit out mistakes or fix shaky footage with the stabilizing effect instead of having to re-shoot everything.

3. Transitions
With transitions, you can move from one clip to the next smoothly and professionally. You can select from a variety of transition options, such as zoom, dissolve, fade-in/fade-out, and many more. The right transition between clips can make a video look better and take it to the next level.

There are different ways to make transitions in movies. Try zooming in and out between shots, adding a cross-fade effect, and other things.

4. Split Edit

Do you need to sync the audio of two different clips that you're joining? With split edit, you can pick the audio track you want for the piece you've cut together and make sure it's in time with the rest of the video. This lets you sync audio without having to do it all at once. For example, you can use it to make a speech or music track that runs over several clips.

5. Flip, Crop, and Rotate

You can easily change the size and direction of a video clip with the flip, crop, and rotate tools. This effect helps a lot of people who make videos, whether they're cutting a bigger picture or video for Instagram or TikTok or flipping the picture so that it looks like a mirror. These three simple iMovie features may not be the sexiest video effects, but they're very useful for making sure that all the details of a video are correct.

6. Day to Night

It can be hard to film movies at night, but iMovie's Day to Night video effect can make it look like it's dark outside. Day to Night is a famous effect that lets you make a scene look like it's nighttime. For decades, filmmakers have used "day for night" to make this effect, and now you can do it yourself with modern video editing tools. You can shoot your videos whenever it works best for you, and then use the "**fix it in post**" tool to turn them from day to night.

7. Filters

When you use filters on your movies, you can change the mood. It's also the fastest and easiest way to fix the colors in your video. You could bring down the brightness of your video by adding a warm tint. Or, with an easy filter, you can make it feel like an old movie or change the mood in many other ways. You also don't have to worry about aligning filters from different apps like Instagram, TikTok, YouTube, and Facebook when you add a filter straight to your video.

8. Dolly Zoom

When you use dolly zoom, the background moves toward you while the things in the center look like they aren't moving. It's hard to get this cool zoom effect in real-time, but it's easy to add in photo or video editing. When you want to add a little extra style to your video or draw all of the viewers' attention to one part of a shot, use a dolly zoom effect.

9. Cutaways

These are shots that show one or more different scenes while the main scene is still going on. Cutaway shots often show flashbacks or another character doing something that is connected to what the characters in the main scene are talking about. You can easily make this video effect in iMovie by putting clips together.

10. Split Screens

Multiple pictures or video clips can be added to a split screen to play at the same time. In a remote roundtable talk, you could use this to show a conversation between two streamers, or you could use it to show a difference between two situations. Musicians use this effect to turn several separate clips into a fun music video. Split screens work well for many types of videos, like group videos, comparison videos, and quick clips for social media.

Make and Use a Green Screen Easily

To easily get the green screen to work well, it's best to use a good camera that can record HD video. But it will work with any camera that can record movies in MP4 and MOV formats, even phone cameras. You will also need good Chroma Key software. There is a lot of it out there, and you can even download some for free. Some programs are **_Final Cut Pro X, Windows Movie Maker 2.0, and iMovie_**. But Chroma Key effects in consumer apps aren't as good. Adobe Photoshop has a built-in tool called "**Chroma Key**" that lets users change the background color of photos that were taken with a green background to anything they want. Some Chroma Key themes are built into a lot of software, and others can be downloaded separately.

How to Make a Green Screen Effect Footage

Method 1: How to DIY A Green Screen Effect Video

Even though you might think so, you don't have to be Peter Jackson or one of the Harry Potter directors to use Green Screen in your movie. A stand, a piece of green sheet that you will be using as a background and a camera that can shoot high-quality video are all that are required.

- **Step 1: Setup**

It's not hard to set up the spot for filming the Green Screen scenes. But before you start putting together your gear, you need to decide if you want to shoot the scene in a studio or outside during the day. It's sometimes best to shoot outside because the sunshine can perfectly light the scene even if you don't have any spotlights. But if you use spotlights in a controlled space, you won't have to worry about shadows or quick changes in light, which will likely let you be more creative.

- **Step 2: Positioning the Green Screen**

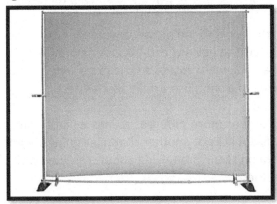

It might seem like a simple step, but if you don't get rid of the wrinkles on the green sheet, you could have a lot of problems after the fact. When you use a piece of paper as your background, make sure it is completely smooth. Even the smallest wrinkle will show up after you remove the background in video editing software.

- **Step 3: Clothes**

They shouldn't wear green costumes in front of a green screen because the editing software will get rid of all the green parts of the shot, including the green parts of the costumes. There are ways to avoid these issues: pick colors that stand out against the blue or green background so you don't have to reshoot the scenes. It's perfectly fine to use clothes that have the same color as the background if you want to make your character see-through.

- **Step 4: Shooting the Green Screen scene**

You can start filming once you've picked the spot, set the lights, and made sure the costume is the right color. To keep your camera from shaking, put it on a stand and make sure it stays still. While the players are acting out the scene, try to pay close attention to every part of the shot. This will help you get better results.

Method 2: Download green screen backgrounds from the website

You can quickly get a green screen for your video by downloading it from a website like *VideoBlocks or Shutterstock*. You can also get free green screen footage in the Filmstock effects store, like the skeleton breaking screen and the scary Sadako ghost. In Filmstock, you can now buy a single piece of green screen footage for a one-time fee.

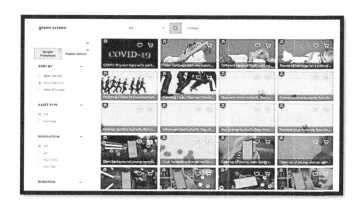

It is possible to get hundreds of different video files with a wide range of motion and other elements that you can use in your movies. If you use already-made Chroma Key footage, you don't have to film it yourself, which can be hard to do if you don't follow all the steps for making Green Screen footage properly. On the other hand, getting footage from websites that sell photos or videos isn't free and can cost a lot. One more thing is that the movies you can download usually only last five or ten seconds.

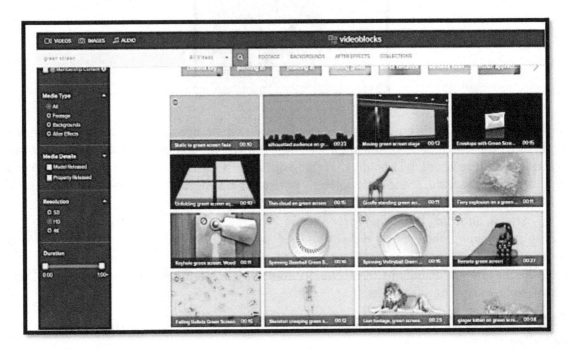

How to Apply Green Screen Effect in iMovie

If you shoot a video with a single-colored background (often green or blue), the iMovie green screen effect lets you make that color see-through. You can choose any other video clip, graphic, or still picture to use as the background. The green screen effect in iMovie makes it easy to add anything to any shot. You can either go anywhere you want or show up in your best movies. How do I use iMovie's green screen? Now do what it says to do to add the green screen effect to iMovie.

Part 1: How to Apply Green Screen Effect in iMovie?

Before you use the green screen effect, make sure you have at least two clips ready: one with the green screen and one with the background.

- **Step 1. Start a New Project**

Go to **File > Import > Movies** on your Mac. This will let you add the green screen and background movies.

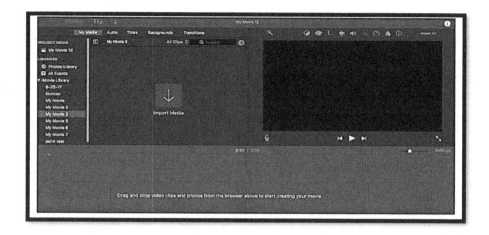

Please make sure that iMovie can play your movies. If not, you won't be able to edit the videos in iMovie. You will need a video converter for Mac to change the videos to iMovie MP4 files so that you can edit them in iMovie. You can drag movies from the **Event** browser to the **Project Library.**

- **Step 2. Drag the Footage into the Timeline**

Once you drag the background clip into the timeline, you can crop, trim, and change this picture or video as you see fit. Once you're done, click on the green screen footage and drag it down to the timeline. Then, put it in the track above the background picture or video.

- **Step 3. Apply the Green Screen Effect in iMovie**

Make sure that both pieces of video are the same length. Within the timeline, click on the green screen footage (a yellow box will appear), then click on **Video Overlay Settings** above the preview window and pick the "**Green/Blue Screen**" option. This is where the real magic takes place.

- **Step 4. Adjust the iMovie Green Screen Effect**

Using the "Softness" and "Clean-up" tools, you can change the effect to make the result better.

How to add filters in iMovie

You need to download iMovie and install it by following the on-screen directions. Then:

1. In iMovie, choose the clip you want to improve and drag it to the editing timeline.
2. Press the "**Filters**" button. A list of filter options will show up.

3. Click on the filter and drag it to the clip you want to use it on. You can remove the filter and drag a new one in its place if you don't like it.

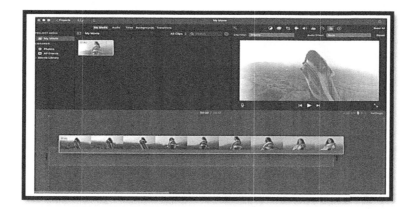

How to Blur Faces in iMovie?

It is hard to blur faces in iMovie, but we will try to explain how to do it in the next part. You will need to use the picture-in-picture tools to hide the face.

Here are the steps you need to take:

- **Step 1.** To begin, open the iMovie app by going to **iMovie > Preferences**. Next, go to **General > Show Advanced Tools** and turn it on. Finally, close programs like iMovie.

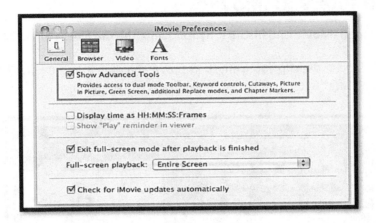

- **Step 2.** Pick the video clip that's shown on the license plate as the first step in the second step. The clip will then be shown in iMovie's player.
- **Step 3:** Press **Shift + Command + 4** to take a picture of the face. Allow the mouse button to go away when you're done. The sound of a shutter will let you know that the screenshot has been taken and saved on your desktop.
- **Step 4:** Open it in an image tool that can blur images, such as **Photoshop or Gaussian**. It can be changed in any way you want. Save your picture to the desktop when you're done making changes.
- **Step 5:** Move it over the iMovie clip and choose **Picture in Picture** from the menu that comes up. The blurred picture will show up as a still in the viewer and iMovie's project pane when you're done with this task.

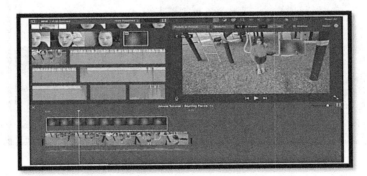

- **Step 6**: Now find the right length of clip to cover the license plate for the whole clip.
- **Step 7**. The last step is to change the image's size and place it where you want it.

CHAPTER 6
INCORPORATING AUDIO

How to Add Audio to iMovie on Mac

Having trouble adding audio to iMovie on a Mac? Import background audio from your Mac into iMovie by following these instructions.

Be sure that the audio and video are well-synced for a perfect product.

- **Step 1:** To add the audio and video clips to iMovie's library, go to **File > Import** Media on the Main Menu. The iTunes library can also be used to import audio files.

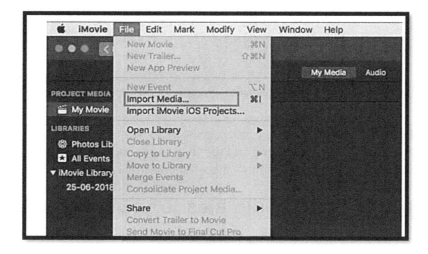

- **Step 2:** All the files you loaded show up under the "MyMedia" tab. Press and hold the audio file you imported and press the spacebar to play it.

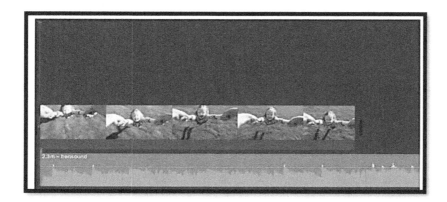

- **Step 3:** Drag the audio file to the timeline and drop it when the **plus sign (+)** goes green. The audio and video might need to be lined up. Click on the audio clip, and when its edge goes gray, moves the slider to cut the video and make it longer or shorter. To add the sound to a certain scene, drag the audio clip to where you want it and let go of the mouse button when the plus sign appears.

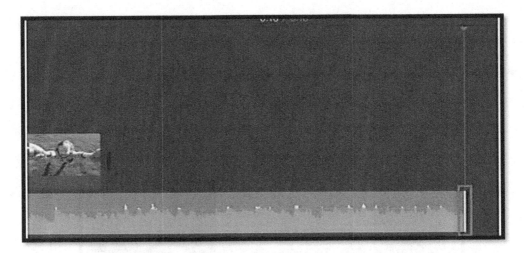

- **Step 4:** Right-click on the audio clip, choose Show Clip Trimmer, and tap Trim to Playhead. This will let you change the volume and speed of the sound and add fade-in and fade-out effects. The options for modifying the imported audio will be found here.

Add songs and other audio files to your iMovie project

Use the Music app to add songs from your library. You can also add other audio files that are on your device, in iCloud Drive, or somewhere else.

Add songs and other audio files on iPhone, iPad, or iPod touch

The Music app on your device lets iMovie access songs from your music library. It can also access audio files saved on your device, in iCloud Drive, or somewhere else.

Add songs from your music library

With the Music app on your Mac, you can sync songs and other audio files from your music library to your device. You can also add songs from your library that you've saved to the Music app on your device.

1. Open your project in iMovie and press the "**Add Media**" button.
2. Click on **Audio**, then **My Music**. Next, click on a group to look through songs.

3. Tap a song to hear a part of it. Please find the song in the Music app and tap the Download button to save it to your device if it is dimmed.

4. Tap the "**Add Audio**" ➕ button next to a song to add it to your project. The song starts at the beginning of the project and is cut to fit the length of the project by iMovie.

You can change the song's length just like you would with any other video. A project can also have more than one song. You can cut the first song in the timeline and then add a different song after it to change the mood of the music throughout your movie.

Add other audio files

You can add audio files from your computer, iCloud Drive, or somewhere else, such as M4A, MP4, MP3, WAV, and AIFF files.

1. If the audio file you want to add is less than a minute long, move the playhead (the white vertical line) to where you want to add the file in your iMovie project's timeline.
2. Press the "**Add Media**" button. Next, press "**Files**" to look through files in iCloud Drive or other places.
3. Click on a file to include it in your project.

When you add an audio file longer than one minute, it works in your project like a song. Files that are less than one-minute long show up where you put the playhead.

Add songs or other audio files on Mac

You can import songs from your music library into the Music app in iMovie for Mac using the iMovie media browser. You can also use the Finder to drag audio files right into your stream.

Add songs or other audio files using the media browser

The media browser in iMovie lets you add songs you've saved to your Mac's music library. It can also be used to add songs and other audio files that are already in your music library.

1. Open your project and click Audio at the top of the window. Then click Music in the Libraries list and look through the options.
2. For a sneak peek of a song, click the play button next to it. You can also pick a song, click on the waveform at the top of the media player, and then press the Spacebar to hear first-hand.
3. **Once you find a song you like, drag it from the media search to the queue:**
   a. To add a song or sound effects to a certain video clip, drag it under the clip until a bar appears that connects the clips. The added song will move along with the video clip if you move it.

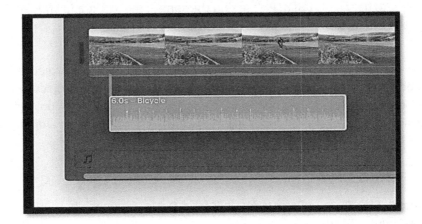

The musical note sign 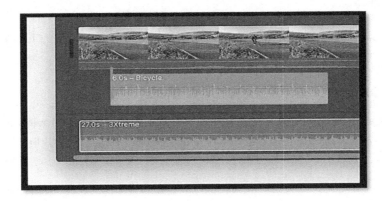 at the bottom of the timeline shows you where the music well is. Drag songs to it to add background or theme music to your movie. You can move video clips around in the timeline, but the song will stay the same.

Choose a range in the waveform at the top of the window so that it has a yellow edge. Then, drag the range to the timeline if you only want to use a part of the song. By dragging on either side of a range decision, you can make it shorter or longer.

Drag audio files into the iMovie project timeline

From the Finder, you can drag audio files like **M4A, MP4, MP3, WAV, and AIFF** files right into your iMovie project's timeline. You can drag files to the music well to add background music, or you can drag the file under a video clip to connect the audio file to it.

If you can't access a song in iMovie

The protected files in your Music library are not accessible and do not show up in the browser. You must either own the rights to a song you bought from the iTunes Store or have permission from the owner of the rights to use it in your project. The iMovie software license agreement can be found by going to iMovie > about iMovie and clicking on License Agreement. It has more information about how to use material in iMovie.

Supported Audio Formats

iMovie supports a wide range of audio formats that you can use in your video projects. Here are the supported audio formats in iMovie:

1. **AAC (Advanced Audio Coding):** AAC is a popular audio format known for its high-quality compression, making it suitable for use in videos without compromising audio fidelity.
2. **MP3 (MPEG Layer-3):** MP3 is a widely used audio format known for its compatibility and small file size, making it convenient for adding background music or sound effects to videos in iMovie.
3. **WAV (Waveform Audio):** WAV files contain uncompressed audio data, preserving the original sound quality. iMovie supports WAV files for high-fidelity audio in video projects.
4. **AIFF (Audio Interchange File Format):** AIFF is another uncompressed audio format that iMovie can import and use in videos. It maintains audio quality but may result in larger file sizes compared to compressed formats.
5. **Apple Lossless:** Apple Lossless, also known as ALAC, is a lossless audio compression format that preserves audio quality while reducing file size. iMovie supports Apple Lossless for high-quality audio in videos.
6. **FLAC (Free Lossless Audio Codec):** iMovie does not natively support FLAC files, which are another lossless audio format. However, you can convert FLAC files to supported formats like AAC or AIFF before importing them into iMovie.
7. **M4A:** M4A is an audio format commonly used for storing music and other audio content. iMovie can import M4A files for use in video projects.

8. **AC3 (Dolby Digital):** iMovie does not support AC3 audio files directly. If you have AC3 audio, you may need to convert it to a supported format like AAC or AIFF before using it in iMovie.
9. **OGG (Ogg Vorbis):** iMovie does not support OGG audio files natively. You may need to convert OGG files to a supported format like AAC or AIFF for use in iMovie projects.
10. **Other Formats:** iMovie may also support other audio formats, depending on the version and compatibility of the software. Always check the latest iMovie documentation or updates for information on supported audio formats.

By utilizing these supported audio formats, you can add background music, sound effects, voiceovers, and other audio elements to your videos in iMovie with ease and maintain high-quality audio throughout your projects.

Best Places to Find Background Music for iMovie

As more people post videos on social media, people who make content look for music that goes well with their videos. Trying to find the right background music can be hard. Hence, we gathered the best web pages where you can discover iMovie background music. These sites can help you find music because they have royalty-free music that you can use in your work without any problems.

iTunes

If you want to find background music for iMovie, iTunes is the best place to go. From top singers, you can find as much high-quality music as you want here. It's important to know the difference between copyright and non-copyright music in iTunes before you use a song in your video.

Spotify

It's hard to not like Spotify. Themed music playlists let you choose music in this app that is becoming more and more popular. You can find a lot of different kinds of instrumental music that would make great background audio.

YouTube

The YouTube library has background music and sound effects that can be used for professional video creation that is free of copyright and royalty issues. Discover some of the best music options for videos online by searching the Audio Library section.

iMovie Audio Editing

Trim Audio Clips

There are a couple of options to trim an audio clip in iMovie.

#1. Trim to Playhead

You can choose where to put the playhead on your timeline. Now, cut an audio file to that exact point. After that, move the playhead and do one of the things below.

- Go to the menu bar and choose **Modify > Trim to Playhead** option.
- Right-click on the audio clip, then choose the **Trim to Playhead** option from the quick menu.

#2. Use the Clip Trimmer

One small part of the clip can be cut off with the Clip Trimmer.

- Right-click on the audio clip and choose "Show Clip Trimmer" from the menu that comes up.
- Once the Clip Trimmer appears, hold down the white lines and drag the arrows to pick the part of the video you want to cut. What will be completely erased is the space between those lines.

It's possible to move the whole clip, but the cut area will stay where it is.

- When you're done with this part, click Close Clip Trimmer.

Shorten or Lengthen Audio Clips

You can easily make an iMovie audio clip longer or shorter. Pick out the pin in the timeline and move one of its sides around. As you carry, the length of the clip will change. And when you're done, a new course will show up in the top left menu. You can also set the exact length of the clip. Right-click on the clip in the timeline and choose "Clip Information." This is the small letter "i" tab above the Viewer. In the white box on the right, type in the number of seconds you want to set the time to.

Change the Speed of an Audio Clip

If you are changing music in iMovie and want to speed up or slow down an audio clip, you can do that. Now, do this!

- **Method 1:** Click the **Speed** button on top of the Viewer. Next, make a choice from the drop-down menu next to Speed and enter a percentage. In that box, you can also change the speed if you'd like.
- **Method 2:** Right-click on the clip and choose "Show Speed Editor" from the menu that comes up. After that, a slider will show up at the top of the clip. You can move it to change the speed.

Change audio volume in iMovie on Mac

When you change a clip's volume in iMovie, the audio waveform changes shape and color to show what you've changed. Check that the waveform's peaks don't show up yellow, which means they are distorted, or red, which means they are cutting, which means they are severely distorted. If your audio waveform is red or yellow, turn down the volume until the whole waveform is green.

If some of the waveform is red or yellow and the rest is green, you can change how loud that part of the waveform is.

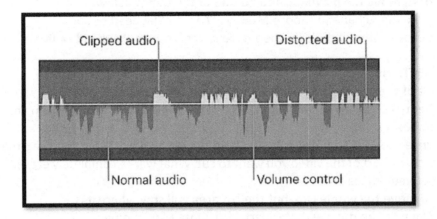

If you don't see waveforms in the timeline, hit the **Settings** button in the top right corner of the timeline and check the box that says To Show Waveforms.

Change volume in a clip in the timeline

1. In the timeline of the iMovie app on your Mac, choose an audio clip or a video clip with sound.
2. Move the bottom line across the audio waveform, which is the volume setting, up or down.

The level shows up as a percentage number as you drag and the waveform changes shape to show how you've changed it.

Change the volume of part of a clip

You can pick a part of a clip and change the volume only for that part. The volume of an audio clip is shown by the black line that runs horizontally through it.

1. Put the pointer over a clip in the timeline in the iMovie app   on your Mac and press and hold the R key. The pointer will change into the **Range Selection pointer** , which you can then use to drag across part of the clip.
2. Drag the volume setting (the line across the waveform) up or down in the range you chose.

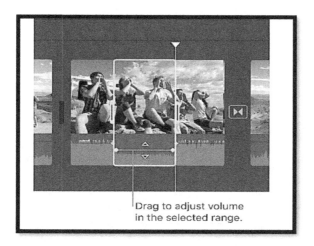

Drag to adjust volume
in the selected range.

Only the volume in the range selection is changed, and iMovie adds a fade to each edge of the selection by itself.

3. Only the volume in the range selection is changed, and iMovie adds a fade to each edge of the selection by itself.

Mute the volume

1. In the timeline of the iMovie app on your Mac, choose one or more audio clips or video clips with audio.
2. Press the Volume button to see the settings for the volume.

3. Press the "Mute" button.
   - Click the Mute button again to turn it off.

Adjust audio over time with keyframes

With keyframes, you can slowly turn up the level on parts of a clip. You can change the volume at certain places in a clip by adding keyframes, which are tiny marks. **The relative volume of an audio clip is shown by the black straight line that runs through it.**

- Open the iMovie app on your Mac and find a clip in the timeline that has audio that you want to change over time.

- Move the pointer to the level control (the horizontal line) in the waveform part of the clip. This is where you want to add a keyframe.
- If you want to add a keyframe, hold down the Option key and click the volume bar.

The pointer turns to the Add Keyframe pointer when you press and hold the Option key while it is close to the volume control. You can click to add as many keyframes to the clip as you want.

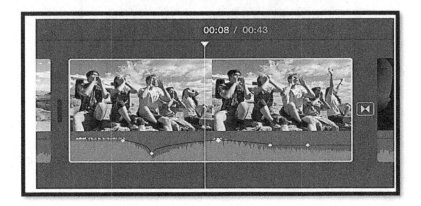

To change the volume of the audio over time, you need to add at least two keyframes to your clip. This is because any volume changes happen between two keyframes.

- **Do one of these things after adding at least two keyframes:**
    - ○ ***Set the volume of the clip at a keyframe***: You can move the keyframe up or down.
    - ○ ***Set the volume of the clip between two keyframes***: You can move the volume pot between the keyframes up or down.

Press and hold on a keyframe in the timeline of a clip to remove it. Then, select remove Keyframe from the menu that appears.

Fade an Audio Clip

If you are editing audio in iMovie, you can also fade the clip in or out. To make a fade-out or fade-in effect, pick a clip in the timeline and then drag the fade handle (a small circle) to the beginning or end of the clip. As you drag, the lines that show the shadows of the clips will fade in and out.

Edit Audio Clips in iMovie on iOS

This is where you sort or arrange all of your audio clips in iMovie. This includes the background music and special effects. In the sequence, audio clips are always below the video clips. You can use the steps below to edit audio clips in iMovie on your iPhones or iPads.

Move an Audio clip

You can move the whole audio clip to a different place, but not the background music.

- With your project open in the timeline, touch and hold the purple or blue audio clip until it goes over the timeline bar.
- Move the clip to a different spot and release.

Adjust the Audio Clip's Duration

- **Step 1:** Open the project in the timeline and tap the blue or purple audio clip or background music clip that you want to change.
- **Step 2:** You can now see the yellow trim handles on the screen. Drag them to where you want the audio to start and stop at the end of the clip. If a cut handle won't move left or right, it just means that the end of that clip doesn't have any more audio to work with.
- **Step 3:** Tap outside of the audio clip to get rid of the trim handles.

Split an Audio Clip

To split audio clips in iMovie, there are typically two options. When you split a clip, you can get rid of parts you don't want or change the length, volume, or speed of each part.

- **Step 1.** Scroll the timeline to where you want to split the audio. This will put your opened project on the timeline.
- **Step 2:** Click on the audio clip to bring up the inspector at the bottom of the screen.
- **Step 3:** Click the "**Actions**" button and pick the "**Split**" tab.

You can also tap the clip to make its edges yellow and then swipe up above the playhead as if you were sliding your finger over it.

Detach the Audio Part from a Video

The video clip's audio can be detached so that it can be edited or deleted as a separate video clip.

- **Step 1.** Open the project in the timeline and choose a video clip. Then, go to the bottom of the screen and open the inspector.
- **Step 2:** Press the "**Actions**" button and then press "**Detach**."
- **Step 3:** A new audio clip in blue will then show up below the video project. Now that the audio clip is separate from its parent video clip, you can move, edit, or remove it.

Move Audio to the Foreground or Background

iMovie suggests audio "ducking" to make sure the sound in your video clips can be heard above the background music. When you duck, the background music clips' noise goes down when there is a video clip playing at the same time.

You can select which audio clips are in the foreground or the background.

- **Step 1:** Click on an audio clip in the timeline to bring up the inspection at the bottom of the screen.
- **Step 2:** Click on the "**Actions**" tab and choose "**Foreground" or "Background**."

Foreground audio (blue or purple) or background music (green) is shown by the clip's color change.

Add Background Music to iMovie Project and Videos

- **Step 1: Build a Project**

To make a new iMovie project, open the one you already have open, click on File, and then choose Import Media. You can either Browse to find the music you need for your project or Type the name of the audio file into the Search field to find it. You can also add song clips straight from your iTunes library.

- **Step 2: Add Background Music**

After finding the music you want to add as background, now it comes to adding background music to videos and projects in iMovie. Drop the music you want to use as background to your iMovie project. Be careful not to drop it on top of a clip. To add background music to the iMovie project, let go of the mouse button when you see the **green plus sign (+).** The background music you added is shown in green, which means it is the background music clip. It starts at the beginning of your iMovie project.

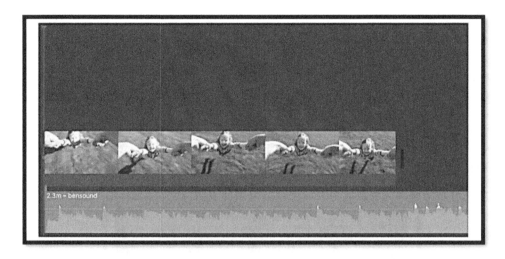

iMovie lets you add background music to parts of video clips by dragging the music to the spot where you want the video to start. Let go of the mouse button when you see the green plus sign (+). You can choose the clip and drag the scale to make the background music longer or shorter while the edge goes gray.

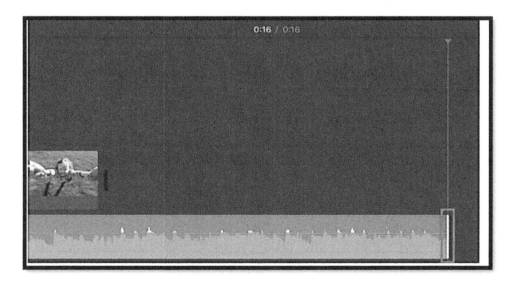

- **Step 3: Adjust Background Music**

You can now change the background music and edit it so that it starts in the middle of the song, for example. Right-click on the background music clip and choose "**Show Clip Trimmer**" > "**Trim To PlayHead**." This will let you change the background music in iMovie. You can cut the song, change the volume, add fade-in and fade-out audio effects, and more.

Part 2: How to Add Background Music to iMovie on iPhone

- **Step 1:** Open the iMovie app and click the "+" button in the top left corner to create a project.
- **Step 2:** Add the movie file from the media to the project.
- **Step 3:** Press the "**Create Movie**" button at the bottom of the screen once the movie is added to the project.
- **Step 4:** Some themes in iMovie can help you make your video look better and fit the right mood. Toggle "Theme music" on the next screen after tapping the gear button at the bottom of the screen. You can now pick the theme you want for your video.

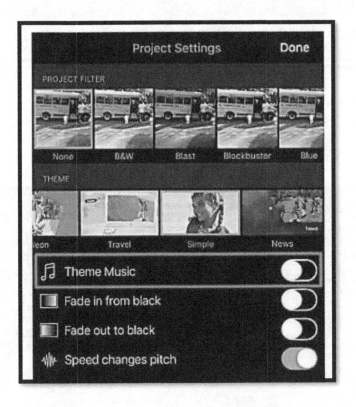

Step 5: Click the "**+**" sign to the left of the video if you want to add your audio and not pick one from the pre-existing collection. Select "**Audio**" and then "**My Music**" on the next screen.

- **Step 6:** Next, pick a song from your phone's Playlists, Artists, Albums, or single songs. Then, hit the "+" button to add it to the video. You can't add more than one song at once. Just add one sound and make the necessary changes.

It's now possible to add the song to the video. You can export the video to your camera or your phone by selecting the "Export" option with the up arrow.

Record and Add a Voiceover in iMovie

You can record audio in iMovie to either add to the movie scenes or make a statement. Why not use this great voice-over feature in iMovie? It is easy to describe a movie and add your voice anywhere in your video by adding audio in iMovie. You can use a built-in microphone or an external microphone.

- **Step 1: Go to the Record Voiceover page.**

Place the Playhead where you want to add the voiceover after adding media to the timeline, and then click the Record Voiceover icon below the sample boxes to start recording.

- **Step 2. Adjust voiceover recording settings**

Now you can adjust the narration recording settings before recording: If you click on the **Voiceover Option** button, you can choose the Input Source you want and change the volume of the speech as well. To change the recording volume, just move the level button to the right or left. If you check the "**Mute Project**" box, iMovie will turn off the music from clips while you record, which a good idea is usually.

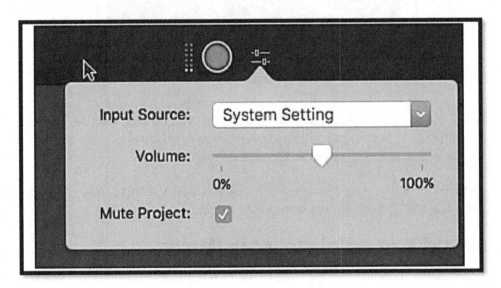

- **Step 3. Start and stop voiceover recording**

To make a video, click the red "**Record**" button. To stop recording, click the Record button again. The voiceover will now show up as a new audio clip in the timeline. When you're done recording the voiceover, click the "Done" button to the right of the settings for recording the voiceover.

CHAPTER 7

WORKING WITH TITLES AND TEXT

Add titles and text in iMovie on iPhone or iPad

You can edit the text after adding it to a video clip, picture, or background in your project. You can add a title scene or end credits to your movie as well.

Add text to a clip

Any video, picture, or background clip in the timeline can have text added to it. You only need to tap the clip, and then tap the Titles button T at the bottom of the screen. Finally, tap a title style.

Edit text

You can change where the title shows up on the screen; edit the text, and more after adding it to a clip. For the title, start your project and tap the clip. Then, tap the Titles button at the bottom of the screen.

You can move the text, edit it, and do other things:

- To edit the text, tap the text in the reader above the timeline, then tap Edit. Type in new text using the keyboard, and then tap Done.
- Drag the text to a different spot to move it.
- To change the size of the writing, pinch it to make it bigger or smaller.

- Tap the text Aa or Color button ⬤ in the preview to change the text style. To view additional letter style options, tap the More button ⬤⬤⬤ .

Any edits you've already made are retained when you change the title style at any time.

1. Open your project and tap on the clip in the timeline. Then tap on the Titles button.
2. Click on a different title type to see what it looks like in the viewer.

Tap the clip, and then tap the Titles button. In the list of title types that come up, tap None to get rid of the text.

Create a title sequence or end credits

You can make a title scene or end credits for your movie by adding a background clip at the beginning or end of it and then adding text to it.

You can use some styles, including cartoon styles, in your movie with iMovie.

- o Open your iMovie project and scroll through the timeline until you reach the beginning or end of the movie.
- o Click the "Add Media" ✛ button and then click "Backgrounds."

- o Choose a background and then click "Add to Project  ."
- o In the timeline, tap the new background clip. Then, at the bottom of the screen, tap the Titles button in the inspector.

- o Click on a type of title. In the reader, the text shows up on top of the stream. Just tap on a different style in the inspector at the bottom of the screen to pick a different one.
- o Cut the background clip to the length you want.

Add text to a clip

Here's how to add text to a video, photo, or background clip in the timeline.

- o Move the playhead to where you want the text to go, click Titles above the window, and then double-click a style.
- o You can also drag the style to the clip where you want it to show up on the timeline.
The text is put as a connected clip on top of the other clip in the frame.

Edit text

You can edit the text after adding it to a clip. You can change the style; move the text around on the screen, and more.
- o Double-click the text-filled clip in the timeline. Type the new text in the viewer. Click the

  Apply button  .

- In the timeline, double-click the clip with the text to change the font type, size, and color. Then, change the font settings at the top of the viewer and click the Apply button when you're done.
- Move your mouse to either side of the clip with the text in the timeline and drag it to change how long it stays in the movie.
- Double-click the title in the timeline, click Titles above the window, and then double-click the new style you want to use. This will change the way the text is placed and how it looks. The new style takes the place of the old one, keeping the length you set and any changes you made to the text.

Create a title sequence or end credits

You can make a title scene or end credits in iMovie using some styles, some of which are animation. If you give your movie a theme, titles that go with it will show up at the top of the window. You can also add a background if you don't want the black background for the title scene.

- Open your iMovie project and click the Media Library button  to bring up the website.
- Put the playhead at the start or end of the movie.
- Click **Backgrounds** and double-click the background you want to use for the title scene or end credits if you don't want a black background. You could also drag the background to the start or end of the file. Move on to the next step if you don't want a background.
    - You can also use any picture or video as the background.
- Click **Titles**, then either double-click or drag the title to the timeline if you want to use it. If you used a background or another clip, the title is added as a connected clip on top of the other clip in the frame. When you move a picture or video clip with a connected clip, the clip moves with it.

Text Formatting Options

- **Font Selection:** iMovie offers a selection of fonts to choose from. Click on the text in the viewer to select it, and then use the Font menu in the text editing toolbar to choose a font style.
- **Font Size:** Adjust the size of the text by using the Font Size slider in the text editing toolbar. Drag the slider left or right to decrease or increase the font size.
- **Font Color:** Customize the color of the text by selecting it in the viewer and using the Color Picker tool in the text editing toolbar. You can choose from a range of colors or enter specific color values.
- **Bold, Italic, and Underline:** Apply formatting styles such as bold, italic, or underline to the text using the respective buttons in the text editing toolbar.
- **Alignment:** Align the text left, center, or right within the text box by using the Alignment buttons in the text editing toolbar.
- **Text Shadow:** Add a shadow effect to the text by selecting it in the viewer and using the Text Shadow button in the text editing toolbar. Adjust the shadow settings, including opacity and distance.
- **Text Outline:** Create an outline around the text for better visibility by selecting the text and using the Text Outline button in the text editing toolbar. Customize the outline color, thickness, and opacity.
- **Background Color:** Apply a background color behind the text to make it stand out. Select the text and use the Background Color button in the text editing toolbar to choose a color.
- **Animation and Effects:** iMovie offers various animation and effects options for text. Select the text and click on the Animation button in the text editing toolbar to choose an animation style, such as Fade In, Pop, or Move.
- **Duration and Position:** Adjust the duration of the text overlay by dragging its edges in the timeline. You can also reposition the text by clicking and dragging it within the viewer.
- **Text Styles:** iMovie includes predefined text styles that you can apply to your text, such as Lower Thirds, Subtitles, Credits, and more. Choose a text style from the Titles browser to apply it to your text.

Previewing and Fine-Tuning

- After applying text formatting, preview the video to see how the text overlays look in the context of your project.
- Make any necessary adjustments to the text formatting, position, or duration to achieve the desired visual effect.

Animate Text in iMovie on Mac

- **Step 1: Download Keynote**

To move on to the next step with iMovie text motion, first get Keynote from the Mac App Store.

- **Step 2: Export video image from iMovie to Keynote**

Move the playhead to the spot in your iMovie project where you want to add moving text. Then, hit the **Share** button and pick the Image. Then it will send this picture as a JPEG, which you need to bring into Keynote. In this case, you need to make a lower-third animation that goes over the picture, get rid of the background, and then export just the animation as a layer to iMovie.

- **Step 3: Remove slide background**

Check to see if you have chosen anything on the slide to remove its background. To get to the No Fill tab, go to **Format > Background**.

- **Step 4: Export lower-third animation as video to iMovie**

To open the Export box, go to **File > Export to > Movie**. When you're done choosing the Self-Playing option, click the **Cancel** tab. After that, go to the "**Animate**" tab, which you can see below. If you click on the **Build Border** tab below, you can now see the Self-Playing settings of the text motion. If you want to use the same resolution settings in iMovie, go back to **File > Export** and choose Custom in the resolution field. After that, you need to pick Apple ProRes 4444 to export the video with a clear background. After that, you need to click **Next > Save As > Export** to move on with iMovie.

- **Step 5: Preview text animation in iMovie**

Move your mouse back to iMovie in Keynote and drag the video file you just saved onto the timeline of iMovie to add it to the top of the other project. This is why you should first think about using the Apple Keynote Presentation bundle to make text move in iMovie. This is because iMovie can't make this kind of video on its own. So, the steps of setting up Keynote, loading files, and saving them are a bit extra here.

Use iMovie Text Effects

How to Add Text Effects in iMovie on Mac

The process is easy to follow with iMovie, even though it doesn't have many options and the products aren't very interesting. You can add different kinds of text templates to movies with iMovie. Each text template has a fixed position and a motion effect. Learn how to add text to an iMovie project to make a dull movie more fun. But first, you need to learn how to use the text effects in iMovie. The Title Text is put in the middle of the screen for the most part. Credits Text and Third Callout are two other types. Third Callouts, like when writing the name of a new person, are usually put at the bottom and to the left or right of the screen. Credit Texts are usually in the middle of the screen. iMovie lets you add text to anything, like the title at the beginning or end of the movie, a character's name at the bottom of the screen, or anything else.

- **STEP 1: Open iMovie and start a new project.**

Pick the Projects tab in iMovie to open the Projects browser. After that, choose Make New and Movie. If you're a regular user, you can also get to an ongoing project like this:

- **Step 2: Add your media**

To add photos, audio, and videos to your project, select the Import Media option. Now, drag the video you just imported to the iMovie timeline, which is the window at the bottom of the screen.

- **Step 3: Add text to the video**

The important part now starts. Click Titles above the browser to open the text window, which is the top window in iMovie. After that, you will have many options. You can see what a text style will look like by moving your mouse over its image.

You can either drag your choice to where you want it to be in the video or double-click it to add it.

- **STEP 4: Create Your Own Text**

You can also make your own iMovie text effect by changing the font style, size, color, and orientation. Double-click the text box to make it changeable, and then type your words in. Then, you can use the tools above the browser to change the font, text size, spacing, character layout, and color of the text until it is the right size and color.

TIP: You can change your text and move it around so it shows in the right place in your video by dragging the text layer to a different area. You can also drag the text overlay box's right or left sides to make it longer or shorter in the timeline.

How to Add Text Effects in iMovie on iPhone/iPad

STEP 1: Launch the iMovie App

On your iPad or iPhone, open iMovie. Tap the **"+"** sign to add the video clip, and then select **"Movie"** from the menu that appears.

STEP 2: Add Text

When you're ready to add text, go to the Timeline of your movie and tap the text button that looks like a **"T"** at the bottom of a clip.

STEP 3: Animate Text:

To add the text you want, double-click on the text box after picking the right text style. In the case of iMovie for iOS, you can choose between Center and Lower to move the words around on the screen of your movie.

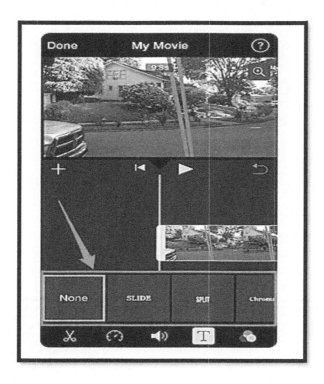

Step 4: Save or share

Finally, click on the Share button below to save or send your iMovie animation text:

Adding Subtitles and Captions

Add subtitles or captions in iMovie on Mac

On a Mac, you can quickly add subtitles or comments to your media when you use iMovie. You do not need any special skills to begin this task. If the video is long, though, it might be good for your fingers.

To begin, you must do the following:

Step 1: Open iMovie.

You need to open iMovie on your Mac before you can start. Look in the Applications folder in your finder window if you can't find the app in the dock. Just double-click the button to open iMovie.

Step 2: Start a new project.

After that, you need to make a new project. You can import the video titles you want to add captions to when you do this. To begin, go to **Project**, then **Create New**, and finally **Movie**.

Step 3: Bring the video in.

To add captions to a video, you must first import it. Pick out the clips you want to use and click on Import Media.

Step 4: Drag and drop videos

The video clip you uploaded will show up in the upper left corner. After that, you can move it to any spot on the timeline you want. You can just drag and drop things here. A small picture of the media file will show up when you click on it. Drag it down to the timeline.

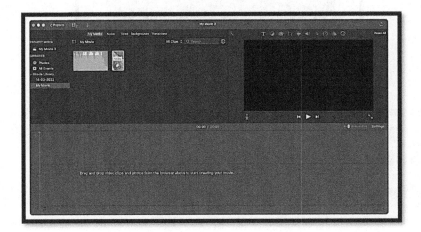

Step 5: Pick the Title style

It's easy to add handwritten notes to iMovie. To begin, click on the Titles button. You will then see a bunch of different style types, such as Split, Expand, Slide, and Focus. Pick the one that fits the style of your brand.

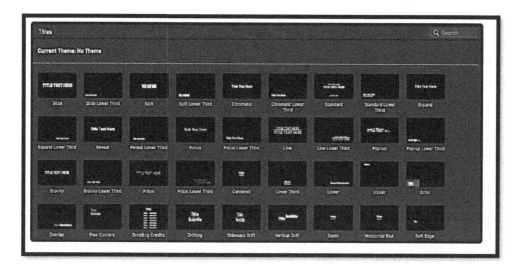

Step 6: Type out your captions

Drag and drop the Title box to the timeline once you've picked a style. You can choose when the subtitles should start. You can put a text box above each video clip, and it will show the time when it was added. For your subtitles, you will need to add more than one. After you've put the Title boxes to the timeline, type your subtitles right into each one. If it works for your video, you can add a few different styles.

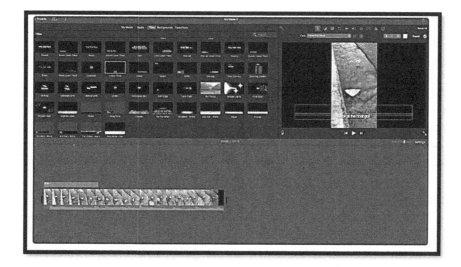

Step 7: Get creative

Once you have written your notes and checked to make sure they are correct, it's time to make things look better. Fortunately, in iMovie, you can edit the words. Pick out a **Title** box and click on it. You will see text options above the video in the top right corner of the screen. Choose the color, style, size, and orientation that work best for your business.

Step 8: Save the video

Save the video is the last thing that needs to be done. Click File at the top of the screen to do that. Press the Share button, then press **File** again. When a box shows up, click Next, give your video a name, and then click **Save**. Plain and simple.

Add subtitles or captions in iMovie on iPhone or iPad

Of course, not every person has a Mac. You can still add subtitles or comments to your video if you only have an iPhone or iPad.

To finish this job, follow these steps:

Step 1: Open iMovie.

To say it again, the first thing you need to do is open iMovie. You can get this app from the App Store if you don't already have it on your iOS device. The app will then open up when you click on the button on your phone. There will be a bar that says "Start New Project" and a few options on it. Pick the Movie option.

Step 2: Import the video

The video to which you want to add captions must first be imported. Please make sure that you have saved a copy of the video on your iPad or iPhone. Once you choose the Movie option at the beginning, the app will take you to the movies on your iOS device. Select the one you want to use by clicking on it and then pressing the "**Create Movie**" button.

Step 3: Put the text in

After that, click on the media in the timeline and then press the **T** button at the bottom of the screen. After you do that, a list of **Title styles** will show up below the timeline. Pick the one that works best for you and move the schedule to the right spot.

Step 4: Type out your captions

The words will show up above the video on the screen. Pick Edit after clicking on it. After that, you can type anything you want into the box. It will show up on top of the video clip at the point you picked when you press "**Play**."

Step 5: Do it again.

You might have to do the steps above more than once if you want to add more than one text to your video. You can pick the same style for the title or find other options.

Step 6: Save the video

Then, click the "**Done**" button in the upper left corner of the screen when you're done. You can save the file by clicking the Share button at the bottom of the screen. You can use WhatsApp or Messenger to send the video to friends, or you can use AirDrop to send it. You can also click "**Save Video**," which will save it to the iOS device you are using at the moment.

How to edit and stylize subtitles in iMovie

We have already talked about how to add subtitles to iMovie. Next, let's talk about how to change them. You will be able to change the text after you have put out your comments. If you're using an iPhone, iPad, or Mac, the process is a little different. Luckily, it's not that hard and won't take long to finish.

How to edit subtitles in iMovie on Mac

You can edit the text after adding subtitles to your video in iMovie on a Mac. There are more options besides the one you will have selected at the beginning.

That being said, here are the steps you should take to change the subtitles on your video.

- Click on the Title box you want to edit.
- Move the mouse to the text options in the upper right corner.
- Click the dropdown menu and pick the font type.
- Use the dropdown to select the font size
- Choose how you want your comments to be aligned.
- Choose from **Bold (B), Italic (I), or Outlined (O).**
- Click on the color box and choose your text color

How to edit subtitles in iMovie on iPhone or iPad

You can edit your videos on this device if you made them on your iPhone or iPad. The process might be a little trickier than you thought.

Here are the steps you need to take after adding the subtitles to your video:

Step 1: Click on the **Title box** you want to edit.
Step 2: Click the "**AA**" button to pick a font style.
Step 3: Pick a font color from the color circle.
Step 4: Click the button to see more options that you can change, such as
- Uppercase or lowercase
- Text shadows
- Text style

To make changes, you can either click on the above options or use the toggle button. Once you've picked the text style you want, all you have to do is click the "Done" button.

CHAPTER 8

INTEGRATING PHOTOS AND GRAPHICS

Supported Image Formats

1. **JPEG (Joint Photographic Experts Group):** JPEG is a widely used image format known for its compression efficiency and compatibility. iMovie supports JPEG images, making them suitable for use as background images, overlays, or graphics in your videos.
2. **PNG (Portable Network Graphics):** PNG is a popular image format that supports transparency and high-quality compression. iMovie supports PNG images, allowing you to use images with transparent backgrounds for overlays, logos, or graphic elements in your videos.
3. **TIFF (Tagged Image File Format):** TIFF is a versatile image format known for its lossless compression and support for high-quality images. iMovie can import TIFF images for use in video projects, maintaining image fidelity and detail.
4. **BMP (Bitmap):** BMP is a basic image format commonly used for graphics and icons. iMovie supports BMP images, allowing you to incorporate bitmap images into your videos.
5. **GIF (Graphics Interchange Format):** GIF is an animated image format that supports looping animations. iMovie can import GIF images, enabling you to use animated GIFs as overlays or visual effects in your videos.
6. **RAW Formats:** iMovie supports certain RAW image formats, depending on the camera model and specifications. RAW formats preserve the original image data without compression, providing maximum flexibility for editing and adjustments.
7. **HEIC (High-Efficiency Image Format):** HEIC is a modern image format used by Apple devices for capturing high-quality images with efficient compression. iMovie supports HEIC images, allowing you to use photos captured in HEIC format in your video projects.
8. **Other Formats:** iMovie may also support additional image formats depending on the version and compatibility of the software. Always refer to the latest iMovie documentation or updates for information on supported image formats.

Image Organization and Management

Image organization and management are essential aspects of maintaining a well-structured and efficient workflow, especially when working with images in iMovie. **Here are some tips and strategies for organizing and managing images effectively:**

1. **Folder Structure:**
   - Create a logical folder structure on your computer to store your images. Organize folders by project name, date, or category to keep related images together.
   - Use subfolders within project folders to further categorize images based on themes, events, or scenes.

2. **File Naming Convention:**
   - Adopt a consistent file naming convention for your images. Include relevant information such as project name, date, location, and a brief description in the file names.
   - Use alphanumeric characters and avoid special characters or spaces that may cause issues when importing into iMovie.
3. **Metadata and Keywords:**
   - Utilize metadata and keywords to add descriptive information to your images. Most image editing software allows you to add metadata like tags, captions, and keywords.
   - Use meaningful keywords that describe the content, context, and themes of your images. This makes it easier to search and filter images based on specific criteria.
4. **Image Editing and Organization Software:**
   - Use image editing and organization software like Adobe Lightroom, Photos for macOS, or Capture One to manage and organize your images.
   - These tools offer features such as tagging, rating, color labeling, and organizing images into collections or albums.
5. **Backup and Storage:**
   - Implement a backup strategy to protect your images from data loss. Use external hard drives, cloud storage services, or backup software to create regular backups of your image library.
   - Store backups in multiple locations to ensure redundancy and data safety.
6. **Tagging and Rating:**
   - Tag and rate your images based on relevance, quality, and usage. Use tags to categorize images by subject, location, people, or events.
   - Assign ratings or labels (e.g., stars or color codes) to quickly identify and prioritize high-quality or key images.
7. **Create Smart Albums:**
   - Many image organization software tools allow you to create smart albums or collections based on criteria such as keywords, ratings, or date ranges.
   - Use smart albums to automatically organize images that meet specific criteria, making it easier to find and manage related images.
8. **Regular Maintenance:**
   - Conduct regular maintenance tasks to keep your image library organized and clutter-free. Delete duplicates, outdated images, and unused files to free up storage space and streamline your workflow.
   - Update metadata, keywords, and tags as needed to ensure accurate organization and searchability of your image collection.

Create a Slideshow with Audio

Step 1: Prepare the Images in Photos

Crop and edit your images in Photos before using iMovie to create slideshows. Then make an album and put the pictures in it so they show up in the slideshow the way you want them to. Even though you can use iMovie to do these things, Photos is a much better choice for editing them.

Step 2: Create a New Project in iMovie

To make a new movie in **iMovie**, open it up and click on the **Projects** button. You have two options in iMovie: you can make a video by combining pictures, videos, and music, or you can make short, fun trailers in the style of Hollywood movies using some of the ready-made themes listed below.

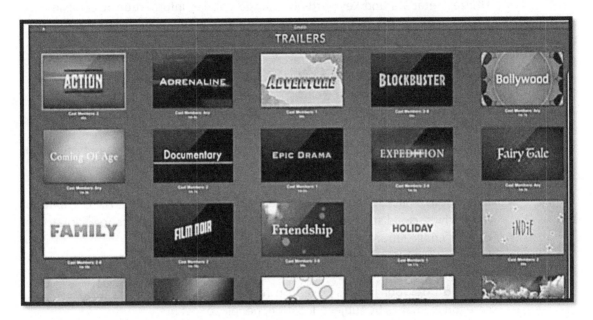

Today, we'll use the Movie tool to make a slideshow because it gives us more options and freedom.

Step 3: Add pictures, videos, and music.

To import your photos, videos, and audio into iMovie, navigate to the **My Media tab** and select **Import**. In the **Photos** app, if you've already organized all of your media, you can just import by going to the Photos tab in the Libraries panel on the left.

Step 4: Adjust the Photos in the Timeline

With the help of the additional edit options found in the Viewer pane, it's time to polish your pictures. You can automatically improve the quality of your pictures with the Magic Wand tool. It can also crop your photos, fix colors, work on color balance, and add effects. Remember to save your changes after making edits.

Step 5: Add Motion to Still Image

It's nice to add motion to still pictures when you use them in a video. Pick out the pictures you want to move, then go to the top of the **Viewer pane** and click on the **Cropping** option. Then, click on the Ken Burns tab. You can change the beginning and finishing frames to make the effect start and stop the way you want it to.

Step 6: Add Transition to Your Slideshow

One of the most important parts of making a smooth video is the transitions. iMovie has many transition effects, such as cross split, fade, and cross blur. If you use a lot of different transitions right after each other, though, it gets confusing and breaks up the flow. Drag and drop it between two pictures in the timeline to add a transition.

Step 7: Add Titles and Text

A great way to show where the beginning and end of your video are is to use titles and text. You can also add some well-known quotes and words to your video to make it more moving. There are several templates you can choose from to add a title. Drop it on the timeline, and now type the words you want to use in the sample window. Since all of the text settings in iMovie include motion effects, you cannot add normal text to your movie.

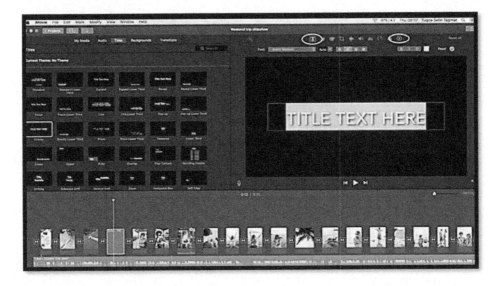

Step 8: Add Music to the Slideshow

As the music for the background of your video, you can either import audio from your computer or get royalty-free music songs from the web. The official iMovie website says that you should buy music from iTunes and then add it to your video. If you're making a video about a story, trim the track to match your slideshow. However, iMovie is not the best option for you if you want to add multiple audio tracks like speech, background music, and sound effects.

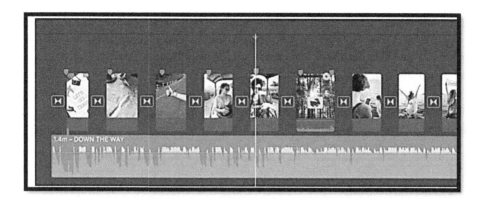

Step 9: Save and Export the Slideshow

Check that everything works by playing the slideshow. To export your slideshow, go to **File > Share > File**. Now you can let your friends see the iMovie video.

For Old macOS Version

If you have an older version of macOS and iPhoto on your Mac, here are the exact steps you need to follow to make a slideshow in iMovie with an iPhoto project.

- **Step 1. Import Photos from the iPhoto Library**

iMovie and iPhoto work together perfectly. To add pictures to the iMovie project, you should drag and drop them from iPhoto. Create a library in iPhoto if one doesn't already exist, then import the pictures. To add videos, go to **"File/Import" or "Event Library"** and drag and drop the movies you want to use to the schedule. You can sample the raw slideshow by hitting the spacebar on your computer after pictures and videos have been added to the iMovie slideshow project. After that, change the clips and transitions. For example, you could move the mouse over a clip or the "double arrow" button and click on the settings icon. This would let you change the settings for the clip, the video, the transitions, and other things.

- **Step 2. Add Music to Your iMovie Slideshow Project**

Project Music makes your slideshow moody. It's as easy to add thoughts to an iMovie display as it is to add pictures and movies. Then, click the **audio button** in the bottom right area and drag and drop the audio file you want to add to the timeline. iMovie could have more than one song added. But iMovie doesn't let you use more than one music. Before adding song tracks into an iMovie video, you may need to use an outside audio editor to join them if needed. An equalizer can be used to reduce sound and add audio effects.

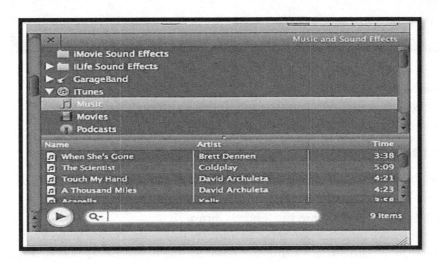

- **Step 3. Export Your iMovie Slideshow Video**

iMovie makes sharing a movie so easy. You can easily post movies to MobileMe Gallery, YouTube, Facebook, Vimeo, CNN iReport, and other sites with iMovie if you want to. If you use Media Browser to share the iMovie movie, the slideshow will also show up in other Mac apps, such as iWeb. It is suggested that you export the iMovie slideshow to iTunes. This way, you can quickly play the slideshow and share it with your iPhone, iPod, or iPad.

Create a Photomontage

1. **Digitize Your Photos**

Each picture you want to use in your photomontage needs to be saved digitally on your Mac before you start putting it together. You're good to go if the pictures are from a digital camera or have already been scanned and saved in Photos. For regular picture copies, use a scanner to turn them into digital files at home. A nearby camera shop should be able to scan your pictures for you if you don't have one or if you have a lot of them. In the Photos app, put all the chosen pictures in one album and name it something easy to remember, like "iMovie album." This will speed up the process of making the montage. If not, you can just look through Photos and pick out any picture you want to use.

2. **Open iMovie**

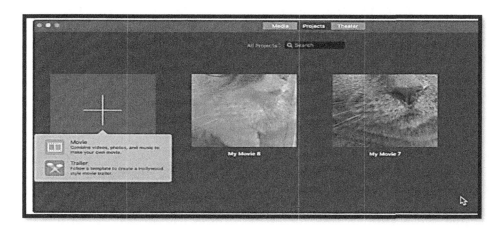

When you open iMovie, go to the File menu at the top of the screen and choose "**New Movie**." You can also press Command + n on the computer to do this. Click the Projects tab and then the big plus sign button next to it in the iMovie screen that comes up. In the window that comes up, pick Movie.

3. **Open the Photos app**

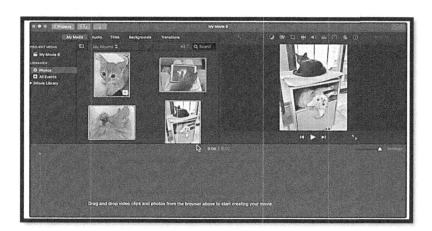

On the iMovie project screen, go to the **My Media tab** and then to **the Libraries part** to the left of the main work area. Click on **Photos**. This brings up the Photos library previews in iMovie, where you can pick the pictures you want to use in the montage from a saved iMovie album or by going through your Photos albums and picking out individual pictures.

4. **Assemble the Photos in the Timeline**

Just click on each picture to pick it out. You can drag the pictures you've chosen to the sequence at the bottom of the screen. You can change the order of the photos by clicking and dragging each one into place.

5. **Go with Ken Burns**

To make the pictures move, use the Ken Burns effect. Choose the first picture and click the crop button at the top of the iMovie window, above the preview screen. This will bring up the Ken Burns settings. Place the Start box and the End box in two different spots on the picture after clicking on them in the viewing window. This needs to be done for each picture. To see the effect, click the play button under the sample window. It might take a while to get it right, but you can change each picture separately until you're happy with the effects. The playhead is the straight yellow line on the timeline. To see how your photomontage effects look, move it to just before the first photo and click the play button under the sample window.

6. **Add a Transition**

You can add other effects to your photomontage if you want to. With transition effects, the breaks between pictures look less abrupt. You can choose from different transitions in iMovie, but the simple **Cross Dissolve** works well with still pictures and doesn't draw too much attention to itself. Get the menu bar and choose **Edit**. Then, pick out all the pictures on the timeline and click on **Add Cross Dissolve**. To see how it looks, click the play button below the sample screen. You can change the time it takes for the cross to fade by hitting the icon that shows up between each picture and typing in a different number of seconds.

7. **Add a Title**

To see examples of different title styles, click the Titles tab near the top of the screen and go to **Content Library > Titles**. Once you choose a title style you like, move the playhead to where you want the title to show in the timeline. This is usually at the beginning. When you double-click your best title style, put the title over the blank text in the sample window. It's now possible to see the title screen.

8. **Fade to Black**

You can click on the Transitions tab or go to **Window > Content Library > Transitions** to open the Transitions menu. By adding a fade-out with the Transitions, the video ends beautifully. So, when the pictures are over, you won't be left with a frozen last frame of video but with a black screen. After the last picture in the collage, add this effect in the same way you did for the title, and the picture will fade away: In the transitions options, position the playhead and tap fade to Black.

9. **Don't forget the Audio**

Once you're happy with how all the pictures and effects look together, add some music to the background of your photos. When you click the Audio tab, a choice of songs will show up. There is a song below the pictures. To add it, click and drag it to the timeline. If the music track goes on for too long, side-scroll to the end, clicks it, and drag it back until it stops right before the last picture.

10. **Last Steps**

Now is the time to test your picture collage. Put the playhead on the timeline just before the first picture. Watch the photomontage from start to finish by clicking the "Play" button under the sample window. This will help you make sure that all of the picture effects, transitions, and titles look good. Now is the time to change anything you see. While you work, iMovie keeps your project. To share your photomontage right away, go to File > Share and choose Email, iTunes, YouTube, or one of the other options. When you click Projects at the top of the iMovie screen, a field will appear where you can type a title. This will take you back to the main iMovie screen.

Create Stop Motion and Time Lapse in iMovie

In some of your video editing projects, stop motion and time-lapse can be fun effects to use. But you might think that to do the job, you need expensive tools or high-end video editing apps. That's not true! If you know how to use it, even iMovie can produce slow video and time-lapse movies.

Here are the steps you need to follow to make a stop motion or time-lapse video in iMovie.

- **Open iMovie**. Go to **Properties>Timing**. "**Fit in Frame**" should be changed from "**Ken Burns**" in the settings. In this way, your pictures will not zoom in and out during the stop-motion effect.
- If your pictures are already in order, all you have to do is click and drag them into iMovie.
- **Adjust the duration of each clip**. Press and hold on to a picture to do this. The inspector window will appear. It should be changed from 4 seconds to 1 seconds. Do this for all of the stills. iMovie will only let you go 10 frames per second, so this will make your stop-motion move at that speed.
- **Export the video**. You can then connect several stop clips if you need to make more than one scene.
- You can add transitions, writing, color correction, and more to your project after you add your stop-motion clip.

CHAPTER 9

MASTERING AUDIO EDITING

Removing Background Noise and Enhancing Audio Clarity

Some Basic Recording-Level Considerations One Should Make to Avoid Noise in Videos

AI has come a long way, and now noise reduction is smooth. There are, however, some things that can be done before recording to reduce noise.

When it comes to noise, the following main things can make a big difference:

1. Pick the Right Location

The first thing you should do when taking audio or video is pick the right place to do it. There is no noise-free place, but people can try. As usual, places with few people and lots of nature don't have noise. You don't have to do much to book a studio for recording audio or video. They provide room and sets that are already planned, as well as noise-canceling gear.

2. Microphone Quality and Position

The microphone is a must-have for making professional-quality audio and video. There is no doubt that a good microphone can produce good sound. An external microphone or a microphone built into the gadget are the two microphone options available. The locations and settings of mics also affect how clear the voice is. The microphone will pick up good words if it is placed closer to the speaker.

3. Protection from wind and interference

People who like to shoot outside have to deal with the noise of the wind. The audio quality gets worse, and watchers find it annoying. Use a shield or a fuzzy cover to cut down on wind noise. To keep the recording from getting other kinds of influence, keep it away from electricity sources. This could include computers, tablets, and other similar gadgets.

4. Audio and Gain Levels

It is important to keep an eye on the audio levels while recording so that they can be made better. Headphones can be used by creators to check audio levels and keep out annoying noises. We also suggest that you set the gain to the right amount for understanding. Through noise and other flaws, a high gain number can reduce audio quality.

5. Right Formats and Editing

Make sure you choose a good audio file before you start recording. The high-quality files that most people use are WAV and FLAC. Besides that, pick the right editing program that can get rid of noise. Also, the program should keep the sound of the audio while changing and afterward. You can also use the audio improvement effects that come with these tools to save the day.

Basic Solution to Background Noise Removal for Mac Users: iMovie

iMovie has audio equalization and audio improvement to make words clearer. With iMovie's audio denoise tool, it's easy to get rid of background noise. The function is built on top of the main writing screen and is simple to use. Also, you can edit audio files in different forms, such as ACC, MP3, and others.

- **STEP 1:** Open iMovie, click "**Create New**," and **import media**. Then, drag and drop your media to the calendar.
- **STEP 2:** Find the menu in the upper right corner and look through the options it has to offer. To begin changing, find the "**Noise Reduction and Equalizer**" button and click it.

- **STEP 3:** Use the options to find the "**Reduce background noise**" slider. You can change the amount of noise reduction by moving this button.

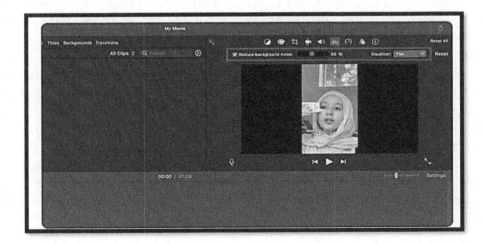

- **STEP 4:** Play your video to see how it turned out and change how loud the noise is. If you're happy with the result, you can export or save the video to iMovie.

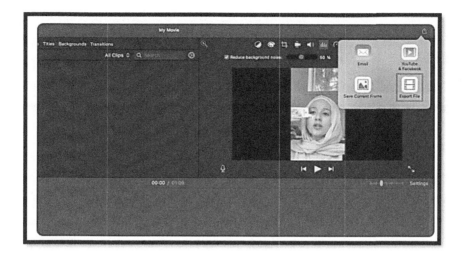

Correct and enhance audio in iMovie on Mac

The audio in your movie can be improved using some tools in iMovie. You can use an equalizer preset, turn down background noise, and boost the volume of quiet audio in a clip.

Automatically enhance audio

1. In the timeline of the iMovie app on your Mac, choose one or more audio clips or video clips with audio.
2. Click the level button to see the level settings.

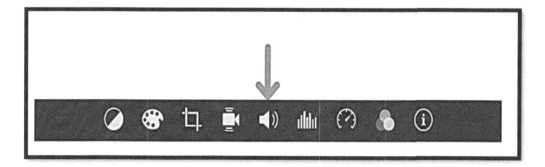

3. Press the "**Auto**" button.

The Auto button becomes underlined to show that automatic improvements have been made, and the average volume of the audio in the selection is increased.

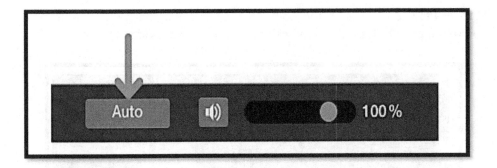

Equalizer Adjustment

You can improve or fix the audio in your movie by using the adjustment settings that come with iMovie. For instance, you can pick a setting for the compressor to improve the quality of the vocals or to boost the bass or sound in a movie.

1. In the timeline of the iMovie app ⭐ on your Mac, choose one or more audio clips or video clips with audio.
2. Click the Noise Reduction and Equalization button to see the equalization settings.

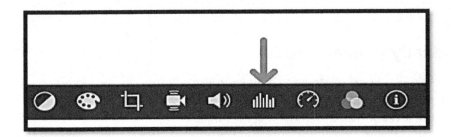

3. Select an equalizer preset from the pop-up window that appears.

Syncing Audio with Video Clips

Part 1. Common Issues of iMovie Audio Out of Sync

The following are the standard issues related to audio out of sync on iMovie:

   1. **Audio out of sync when creating a video**

I made a video for my social media account with iMovie. The audio is still not in sync with the video even after trying different fixes. I read that you should disconnect and reconnect, but that didn't help me either! I finally found something strange: all of these pieces said that my problem would be fixed if I split long movies into several clips and then removed the sound from each one.

   2. **Audio out of sync when exporting an edited video**

I am having trouble getting my recorded lecture to work with iMovie. How can I get the two to work together perfectly so that when I export them, they will play back together?

3. Import video from iPhone to Mac having an audio/video sync problem in iMovie

How are you? I'm editing movies on my macOS X computer with the newest version of iMovie. But the audio and video from the iPhone don't match right. If you use the main camera or FaceTime, the file plays back at different speeds. This means that there was a time mistake while recording, which makes them lose sync when you import them into Apple Final Cut Pro. Why do I need to know what the trouble is?

4. Audio out of sync when importing camera video to iMovie

I'm having trouble getting the audio and video on my laptop to sync with the latest version of Mac OS when I switch from camera tapes. The first thirty seconds or so are exactly in time, but after that, movies that have been moved start moving by three to six seconds! Now, what does this seem to be because of?

Part 2. Easy 4 steps to sync audio and video iMovie

Check out the steps below to learn the various ways you can sync audio and video using iMovie:

1. Extract Audio and Edit it

You can remove the audio from a video in iMovie and edit it separately. The steps below should help you if you don't know how to do that exact move:

- Open iMovie and go to the menu bar. Then, click on File. Import the video you want to edit by clicking Import Media there.
- To export the audio, next choose the clip you just added and click "Detach Audio."
- Now, right-click on the audio files in the timeline and choose "Edit." Press Trim to Selection and make any necessary changes based on the video.
- Finally, click **File** and **Save** to finish making the changes.

2. Add External Audio to Video with iMovie

The steps are listed here:
- Open the video in iMovie that you want to sync.
- Now, drag the video and audio files to the timeline in iMovie.

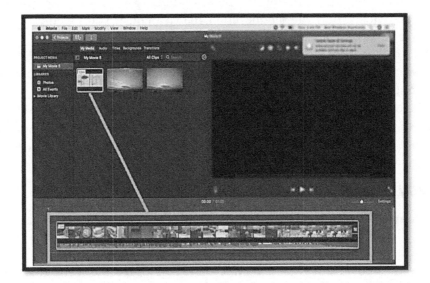

- After that, select Video and turn off the Speaker option to get rid of the audio.
- After that, add the audio file you took out back to the timeline and make sure it is in sync with the video.

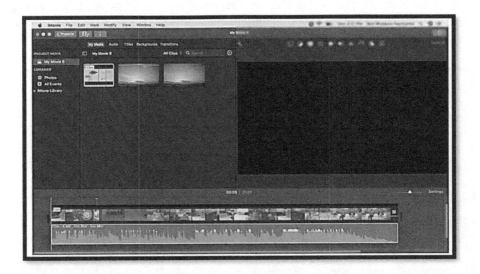

- To save the video, click **Share** and then **Export File**.

CHAPTER 10
EXPORTING AND SHARING PROJECTS
Exporting Projects in Different Formats and Resolutions

Exporting projects in different formats and resolutions in iMovie allows you to customize the output to suit various playback devices, platforms, and quality requirements.

Here's a guide on how to export projects in different formats and resolutions in iMovie:

1. **Open Your Project:**
   - Launch iMovie on your Mac and open the project you want to export.
2. **Select Export Options:**
   - Click on the "File" menu in the menu bar at the top of the screen.
   - Choose the "Share" option from the dropdown menu.
3. **Choose Export File Format:**
   - In the Share menu, select the "File" option to export your project as a video file.
   - A dialog box will appear with export settings. Choose the desired file format for your export, such as MP4, MOV, AVI, or others, depending on your playback requirements.
4. **Adjust Resolution and Quality:**
   - In the export settings dialog box, you can adjust the resolution and quality of the exported video.
   - Select the "Resolution" dropdown menu to choose the desired resolution. Common options include 1080p (Full HD), 720p (HD), or custom resolutions.
   - Use the quality slider or dropdown menu to set the export quality. Higher quality settings result in larger file sizes but better video quality.
5. **Customize Video and Audio Settings (Optional):**
   - Depending on the selected file format, you may have additional options to customize video and audio settings.
   - For example, you can adjust video codec, frame rate, bitrate, audio codec, and audio bitrate for more control over the export settings.
6. **Choose Export Location:**
   - After customizing the export settings, click on the "Next" button to proceed.
   - Specify the export location where you want to save the exported video file on your computer.
7. **Export and Save:**
   - Click on the "**Save**" button to start exporting your project with the selected settings.
   - iMovie will process the project and create the exported video file based on your chosen format, resolution, and quality settings.

8. **Additional Export Options:**
    - iMovie also offers other export options such as sharing directly to social media platforms like YouTube, Vimeo, Facebook, and more.
    - You can also export projects for specific devices like iPhones, iPads, Apple TVs, or DVDs if needed.

By following these steps, you can export your iMovie projects in different formats and resolutions tailored to your specific needs, ensuring optimal playback quality and compatibility across various devices and platforms.

Export Settings Customization

Understanding iMovie Export Settings

Before you decide to export movies from iMovie to another device, you need to start here. Because the settings affect important things like compatibility and file size, they should be given full attention. It will be hard to export movies from iMovie if you don't understand how these settings are used. Because of this, make sure you read them all one by one. One important thing you will learn is how easy it is to change these settings to suit your needs.

When people export movies from iMovie, they most often use QuickTime. This is a good example of how to change the settings. Going to the "file" tab and choosing "**export**" will do that. Then, a choice with all the types will appear. In that case, pick "expert settings" and then click the "**export**" button. "**Movie to QuickTime movie**" will also be an option on the pop-up menu. Press the "options" button to see more choices. The "settings" button will be easy to see. Clicking it will bring up a video panel with information on compression, frame rate, and other important settings. Pick the right settings for adjusting based on your tastes. In the end, you should choose customization options that give you a good return in terms of file size and clarity. The only way to get the most out of your iMovie settings is to do that. If you mess up any of the settings, it will affect the quality of your movie and make exporting harder. So that everything is the same, you will need to put the frame size first, then the frame number, and finally the frame rate.

Resolution and Quality Considerations

Concerns about size and quality are very important when exporting movies from iMovie because they affect how the downloaded video looks and plays. **When uploading movies from iMovie, here are some important things to keep in mind about size and quality:**

1. **Resolution:**
   - **1080p (Full HD):** This resolution, also known as 1920x1080, is suitable for high-definition playback on most modern devices, including TVs, monitors, and online platforms like YouTube.
   - **720p (HD):** With a resolution of 1280x720, 720p is a good choice for HD playback on devices with smaller screens or lower bandwidth capabilities.
   - **Custom Resolutions:** iMovie allows you to specify custom resolutions based on your specific requirements. Custom resolutions are useful for projects with unique aspect ratios or specialized playback needs.

2. **Quality Settings:**
   - **High Quality:** Choosing higher quality settings results in larger file sizes but maintains better visual fidelity and detail in the exported video. This is ideal for professional projects or videos where image quality is paramount.
   - **Medium Quality:** Medium-quality settings strike a balance between file size and visual quality, making them suitable for general-purpose videos or online sharing.
   - **Low Quality:** Lower quality settings reduce file sizes but may result in visible compression artifacts or reduced clarity. Use low-quality settings sparingly, such as for quick previews or drafts.

3. **Bitrate and Compression:**
   - **Bitrate:** Higher bitrates result in better video quality but also lead to larger file sizes. Adjust the bitrate settings based on the desired balance between quality and file size.
   - **Compression:** Video codecs and compression algorithms impact how efficiently the video is compressed without sacrificing too much quality. Choose codecs and compression settings that offer a good balance between compression efficiency and visual fidelity.

4. **Playback Compatibility:**

- Consider the target devices and platforms where the exported video will be played. Ensure that the chosen resolution and quality settings are compatible with the playback capabilities of these devices.
- For example, older devices or slower internet connections may struggle with high-resolution or high-bitrate videos, leading to playback issues or buffering.

5. **File Size Management:**
   - Large file sizes are suitable for preserving video quality, but they may pose challenges in terms of storage space, upload/download times, and playback performance.
   - Optimize file sizes by balancing resolution, quality, and compression settings to meet your needs while keeping file sizes manageable.

6. **Testing and Previewing:**
   - Before finalizing the export settings, preview the video in iMovie to ensure that the resolution, quality, and visual appearance meet your expectations.
   - Conduct playback tests on different devices and platforms to verify compatibility and assess how the exported video performs in real-world scenarios.

Uploading Videos to Social Media Platforms

Share to social platforms in iMovie on Mac

You can get your movie ready to post on famous websites that let people share videos.

1. Open the iMovie app on your Mac and choose a movie, video, or clip from the list.
2. Click on **File**, then **Share**, then **Social Platforms**.
3. **In the next window, choose one of the options given:**
   - *Set the title of the shared movie:* Click the name at the top, and type a new name.
   - *Set the description of the shared movie:* Click in the Description field, and type new text.
   - *Set tags for the shared movie:* Click in the Tags field, and type tag names separated by commas.
   - *Set the resolution of the shared movie:* Click the Resolution pop-up menu and choose an option.
   - *Speed up the export with simultaneous processing*: Check the box next to "**Allow export segmentation**" to speed up downloads of projects that take three minutes or more. iMovie sends parts of your video to available media engines so that they can work on them at the same time.

Note: You need at least macOS Sonoma and an Apple M1 Max, M1 Ultra, M2 Max, M2 Ultra, or M3 Max on your Mac to export segments.

4. Click the **next** button.

5. Give the output media file a name, choose where on your Mac or storage device you want to save it, and click **Save**.

The way your project is saved makes it easy to share on social networks.

On the right side of the menu, there is a progress bar. To see more information, click the progress bar. When the process is done, the sign goes away.

6. Use an online browser like Safari and follow the guide on the website or app to share the file.

Using AirDrop with iMovie on iOS

You can use AirDrop with iMovie on iOS in two different ways. You can share single video clips or an iMovie project (like a movie or a trailer) along with all the video files that were used in it. **To send separate video clips:**

1. Make sure AirDrop is turned on for both devices.
2. Select the video you want to share in iMovie's video browser and tap it.
3. Press the "Share" button.
4. Tap the device you want to receive the video clips from the list of close devices that have AirDrop turned on.

The process of sending the video clips will begin. If the names of the devices don't show up, make sure that AirDrop is turned on for all nearby devices and that all of them are in the Contacts app or your AirDrop settings are set to "Everyone."

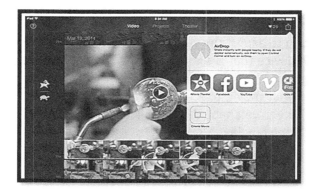

5. Tap **Accept** on the warning that shows up on the device that is getting the video clips. The received device's Camera Roll is updated with the video clips.

Share or export your iMovie project on iPhone or iPad

You can email or text your movie, exports it so you can watch it on another device, or post it on the web. Open the saved project in iMovie, make your changes, and then share your movie again when you're done if you want to edit it after sharing it.

Send your movie via email or text message

With the Mail app or the Messages app, you can send a finished movie to someone in an email or a text message.

1. Select the movie you wish to share from the Projects list. Tap "**Done**" in the top left corner to finish changing a project.
2. Press the **Share** button ⬆️, and then press **Messages or Mail**.
3. Finish the email or message that was made, and then press "**Send**."

You can make the movie file smaller if it's too big to send. Stop the email or message you're reading, go back to the share screen, tap Options, and then pick a smaller size.

Export your movie to watch on another device

You can use AirDrop to send the movie file to another close Apple device so you can watch it. Your movie can also be saved to your Photos library.

1. Select the movie you wish to share from the Projects list. Tap "Done" in the top left corner to finish changing a project.
2. Press the "Share" button.
3. Tap Options, then tap Done when you've selected your options to change your movie's size or format.
4. **Select the destination for your movie's export:**
   o To use AirDrop, press the "**AirDrop**" button and then tap the user's picture at the top of the screen. Apple users can also use AirDrop to send files to each other.
   o Tap **Save Video** to export the video to your Photos library. You can watch the video on any Apple device that is signed in to the same iCloud account if you have iCloud Photos turned on.
   o You can save your movie to iCloud Drive, a folder on your device, or a third-party storage service you've enabled in the Files app. To do this, tap **Save to Files**, pick a location, and then tap **Save**.

Share your movie on the web

First, save your movie to the Photos library. Then, put it on the web.

1. Open iMovie and go to the Projects tab. select the project you want to share. Press the **Share** button.
2. Tap **Options** under the movie title, and then pick a quality if you want to change the size of your video. You can share videos on the web in 1080p.
   - Lower resolutions, like 720p HD, make files that are smaller and can be uploaded to the web more quickly than movies with higher resolutions.
3. Tap "**Save Video**" to save your movie to your device's Photos library.
4. Get off your phone and open an app like YouTube or Facebook. Or, go to the website of the service you want to use and share your video there.

Share or export your iMovie project on Mac

You can email your movie, save it to your Photos library, or get it ready to share online. Open the saved project in iMovie, make your changes, and then share your movie again when you're done if you want to edit it after sharing it.

Send your movie via email

With the Mail app, you can share your movie with other people.

- Pick out the iMovie project you want to send in the Projects window. Then, hit the "**More**" button and pick "**Share Project**." Just click the **Share button** if you're editing a project.
- Click on **Email**.
- Click on **Share**. You'll see a message on the share screen if your movie file is bigger than the suggested size, which is generally 10 MB.

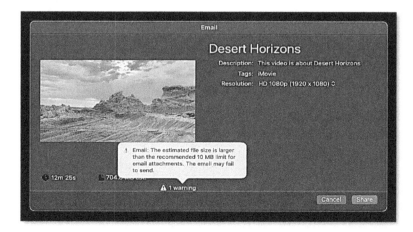

- When you open the pop-up menu, click Resolution. Pick a resolution that makes the movie file smaller than what most mail systems can handle.
- Click on Share. You'll receive a notice once iMovie has finished sending the movie to email.
- Fill out the email that was made, and then click "Send."

Add the movie to your Photos library

You can add the movie to your Photos library, store it in iCloud Drive, or save it somewhere else after you save it as a file. **You should also save the movie as a file if you want to email it using a different email program or service.**

1. Pick out the iMovie project you want to send in the Projects window. Then, hit the "**More**" button and pick "**Share Project**." Just click the Share button while you're editing a project.
2. Click on **File**.
3. Pick a size for your video from the Resolution window that appears. The quality that comes with your movie determines what size it is. When you choose a lower quality, the file is smaller and takes less time to post to the web. If you choose a better quality, the file will be bigger, which is great for watching on a Mac or an HDTV through Apple TV.
4. Pick a place to save the video file, then click "**Save**."
5. Drag the movie files you just saved into the Photos app to add it to your library of photos. You can watch the video on any Apple device that is signed in to the same iCloud account if you have iCloud Photos turned on.

Share your movie on the web

iMovie has settings that make it easy to share on Facebook and YouTube. You can also use this setting to easily share to other websites, such as Vimeo and Twitter.

1. Open your project in **iMovie** and click the **Share** button.
2. Click on **Facebook** and **YouTube**.
3. Pick a place to save the video file, then click **Save**.
4. Open your web browser and go to the site where you want to share your video. Then, post the video file.

CHAPTER 11

COLLABORATIVE EDITING WITH ICLOUD

Setting up iCloud for Collaborative Editing

Setting up iCloud for collaborative editing in iMovie allows multiple users to work on the same project simultaneously, share media assets, and collaborate seamlessly.

Here's how you can set up iCloud for collaborative editing in iMovie:

1. **iCloud Account:**
   - Ensure that each collaborator has an iCloud account and is signed in on their Mac or iOS device.
2. **Enable iCloud Drive:**
   - On each collaborator's Mac or iOS device, go to System Preferences (Mac) or Settings (iOS).
   - Navigate to iCloud settings and ensure that iCloud Drive is enabled.
3. **Save iMovie Project to iCloud:**
   - Open your iMovie project on your Mac.
   - Click on the "File" menu and select "Move to iCloud" or "Save to iCloud" (the exact wording may vary depending on your iMovie version).
   - Choose the location within iCloud Drive where you want to save the project.
4. **Share Project:**
   - Once the project is saved to iCloud, click on the "Share" button in iMovie.
   - Select the "Share Project" option and choose "iCloud" as the sharing destination.
   - Invite collaborators by entering their iCloud email addresses or Apple IDs.
5. **Collaborative Editing:**
   - Collaborators can access the shared iMovie project from their Mac or iOS device by opening iMovie and selecting the project from the iCloud section.
   - Multiple users can work on the same project simultaneously, making edits, adding media, and refining the project collaboratively.
6. **Syncing Changes:**
   - iCloud automatically syncs changes made by collaborators in real-time, ensuring that everyone has the latest version of the project.
   - Collaborators can see each other's edits and contributions as they work on the project together.
7. **Communication and Coordination:**
   - Use communication tools like messages, emails, or project management platforms to coordinate tasks, discuss changes, and keep everyone informed about the project's progress.

- Communicate effectively to avoid conflicts, overlapping edits, or misunderstandings during collaborative editing.

8. **Backup and Versioning:**
   - iCloud provides automatic backups and versioning for iMovie projects, allowing you to revert to previous versions or restore deleted content if needed.
   - Encourage collaborators to save their work periodically and back up important files to iCloud to prevent data loss.

iCloud Account Configuration

1. **Sign in to iCloud:**
   - On your Mac, go to System Preferences.
   - Click on "**Apple ID" or "iCloud**" depending on your macOS version.
   - Sign in with your Apple ID and password.

2. **Enable iCloud Drive:**
   - In System Preferences, select "**Apple ID" or "iCloud**."
   - Check the box next to "iCloud Drive" to enable iCloud Drive syncing.

3. **iMovie Preferences:**
   - Open iMovie on your Mac.
   - Go to the iMovie menu and select "**Preferences**."
   - In the Preferences window, click on the "**General**" tab.

4. **Choose iCloud as Storage Location:**
   - In iMovie Preferences, under the General tab, locate the "Library Location" section.
   - Choose "**iCloud Drive**" from the dropdown menu as the storage location for your iMovie Library.

5. **Save Projects to iCloud:**
   - When creating or saving a new iMovie project, choose iCloud Drive as the destination.
   - Click on "**File**" in iMovie, then select "**Move to iCloud" or "Save to iCloud**" to save the project to iCloud.

6. **Share Projects via iCloud:**
   - To collaborate on iMovie projects using iCloud, click on the "Share" button in iMovie.
   - Choose "**Share Project**" and select "**iCloud**" as the sharing destination.
   - Enter the iCloud email addresses or Apple IDs of your collaborators to invite them to collaborate on the project.

7. **Collaborate and Sync Changes:**
   - Collaborators can open the shared iMovie project from their iCloud Drive on their Mac or iOS devices.
   - Make edits, add media, and work collaboratively on the project.
   - iCloud automatically syncs changes in real-time, ensuring that everyone has the latest version of the project.

8. **Backup and Versioning:**
   - iCloud provides automatic backups and versioning for iMovie projects, allowing you to revert to previous versions if needed.
   - Encourage collaborators to periodically save their work and back up important files to iCloud to prevent data loss.

Sharing Projects

Share iMovie Projects on iCloud

Method 1: Share directly from iMovie

- **Step 1: Open your iMovie project**

Open iMovie on your phone or tablet and start the project you want to share. Before moving on, make sure all edits have been made.

- **Step 2: Click "Share"**

Find the "**Share**" option in the top menu bar and click on it. A drop-down choice with different sharing options will show up.

- **Step 3: Pick "File"**

Find the sharing options and choose "File." This will bring up a window where you can change the settings for the iMovie project you saved.

- **Step 4: Choose iCloud Drive as the location.**

Choose iCloud Drive as the place where you want to save your iMovie project in the file export window. To organize things, you can either make a new group or choose a current one.

- **Step 5: Click "Next" and "Save"**

Simply click "**Next**" to make sure your export settings are correct. After that, click "**Save**" to start the export process. Now, iCloud will store your iMovie project, and any device that is linked to your iCloud account will be able to view it.

Method 2: Use iCloud Photos to Share iMovie Videos

- **Step 1: Export your iMovie project as a video file**

Export your iMovie project as a video file before moving any further. Follow the steps in Method 1, but make sure the video file works with iCloud Photos.

- **Step 2: Open iCloud Photos on your device**

Open the Photos app on your computer to get to iCloud Photos. Make sure you are logged in with the same Apple ID that is tied to your iCloud account.

- **Step 3: Upload the iMovie video**

In iCloud Photos, click the "**+**" or "Upload" button and choose the iMovie video that you saved. You will get the video in your iCloud Photos library.

- **Step 4: Share the video link**

Find the video in your iCloud Photos library after you've posted it. To make a link that can be shared, click on the share button and select the option. This link can be given to anyone who needs to see your iMovie project.

Method 3: Collaborate via Shared iCloud Folder

- **Step 1: Open iCloud Drive**

Use your device to get to iCloud Drive. Make sure that iCloud Drive is turned on in your device's settings if you don't already have the iCloud Drive app.

- **Step 2: Make a New folder.**

You can make a new folder in iCloud Drive just for your iMovie projects. To start making a folder, right-click or tap the "+" button.

- **Step 3: Share the folder**

Select the option to share by right-clicking the newly formed folder. You can send invites, enter the email names of people who will be working with you, and set their entry rights.

- **Step 4: Add iMovie projects to the shared folder**

You can put your iMovie projects in the shared folder by dragging and dropping them. The ability to view and edit the folder's contents will be available to all partners with access, fostering efficient teamwork.

Method 4: Share via iCloud Link

- **Step 1: Export the iMovie project**

Follow the steps in Method 1 to export your iMovie project, and choose iCloud Drive as the location.

- **Step 2: Locate the exported project in iCloud Drive**

Find the folder on iCloud Drive where you saved your iMovie project after exporting it. Click the project file right-click.

- **Step 3: Create a shareable link**

Choose the option to make a link that can be shared. iCloud will give you a link that you can copy and send to other people.

- **Step 4: Share the link**

Put the link in an email, text message, or any other way you like to talk to people to share the iMovie project. The project can be accessed by clicking on the link that was sent.

Collaboration Communication Channels

When collaborating on projects in iMovie or any other creative endeavor, effective communication channels are essential for smooth workflow, coordination, and sharing of ideas.

Here are some communication channels you can utilize for collaborative editing in iMovie:

1. **Email:**
   - Email is a traditional but effective way to communicate with collaborators. Use email to share project updates, discuss changes, and provide feedback.
   - Create dedicated email threads for project-related discussions to keep conversations organized.
2. **Instant Messaging Apps:**
   - Utilize instant messaging apps like Slack, Microsoft Teams, or Discord for real-time communication and quick collaboration.
   - Create project-specific channels or groups within these apps to facilitate discussions, share files, and coordinate tasks.
3. **Video Conferencing:**
   - Schedule regular video meetings using platforms such as Zoom, Google Meet, or Microsoft Teams.
   - Conduct brainstorming sessions, review project progress, and discuss ideas face-to-face (virtually) with collaborators.
4. **Project Management Tools:**
   - Use project management tools like Asana, Trello, or Monday.com to track tasks, set deadlines, and assign responsibilities.
   - Collaborators can use these tools to communicate about specific project tasks, updates, and milestones.
5. **File Sharing Platforms:**
   - Leverage file-sharing platforms such as Google Drive, Dropbox, or OneDrive to share project files, media assets, and resources.
   - Collaborators can access and collaborate on shared files, including iMovie project files, videos, images, and documents.
6. **Collaborative Editing Tools:**
   - Consider using collaborative editing tools designed for creative projects, such as Frame.io, Wipster, or Adobe Creative Cloud collaboration features.
   - These tools allow real-time collaboration on video projects, including sharing feedback, making annotations, and reviewing edits.
7. **Feedback and Review Platforms:**
   - Use platforms like Vimeo (with review and approval features), Screenlight, or Notion for collaborative feedback and review of video projects.
   - Collaborators can leave comments, annotations, and suggestions directly on the video timeline for efficient review and revision.
8. **Documenting Decisions:**
   - Maintain clear documentation of decisions, feedback, and project updates using shared documents, spreadsheets, or project wikis.
   - Documenting decisions helps keep everyone informed and ensures continuity throughout the project.

CHAPTER 12

USING IMOVIE EFFECTS – OVERLAYS AND KEYFRAMING

Cutaways – introducing overlays in iMovie

One clip on top of another is called an overlay. After Effects in iMovie are not their track; they are linked to other media. This means that overlays:

- Don't move to the side when you move a clip over them; in fact, they get erased because you can only have one connected video at a time;
- Don't move to the beginning of the project.

Both iOS/iPadOS and macOS have overlays that can be used in Movie mode. However, overlays are made in different ways in each version. You will need a clip in the timeline before you can add an overlay. Now, let's talk about how to add a clip as an overlay.

For iPhone/iPad:

- Select the media you want to use as an overlay in the Media Browser.
- Press the three dots next to the play button.
- Pick the kind of video overlay you want to use.

If you want to change the type of overlay after adding the clip, tap on it and choose Overlays from the menu below the timeline.

For macOS:

- Pick out a clip to use as an overlay in the Media Browser.
- Press Q or drag it on top of a clip in the timeline.
- The media that is linked will automatically use the Cutaway overlay type. The Video overlay settings button is on the left side of the menu. Click it to change the type of overlay:

Both versions of iMovie offer the same four types of overlay:

- Cutaway
- Split Screen
- Green/blue screen
- Picture in Picture

You are most likely to use the cutout type of overlay when you are changing. Cutting away can add meaning or hide problems in different ways, which is why they show up so often.

Using cutaways to hide jump cuts

A cutaway sits on top of and obscures the clip below it. They are often used to hide cuts and breaks in editing and make a scene look a lot better than it is. You can't cut the video in half if you talk to the camera for a few lines, pause, and then say one more sentences before pausing again. If you do that, the video you get will be jumpy because you'll be moving around a lot as you go from hesitating to speaking. It will get old to watch. It will also be much easier to tell that the words you're speaking are separate from each other because the images will move in a way that doesn't make sense. This will make what you say harder to understand as a whole. But if you put a split on top of all the jumps in the video, the audience will only see one smooth shot. This will make the sentence and the video move much better. Cutting to a shot that doesn't show the face of the speaker lets you crossfade and reduce the audio without worrying about showing the cuts.

There are different kinds of cutaways, such as the ones below:

- **B-Roll:** footage that fits with the story you're telling but doesn't show what's being said directly. It shows how what's being said fits into the bigger picture. One example would be a picture of a computer while a critic talks about its tech specs.
- **Reaction shots**: These show the story from a different point of view. People who stare, nod, or shake their heads could be doing this while someone else talks. A method called "shot/reverse-shot" lets you switch between two shots of a talk.
- **A better take**: You could use a cutaway to go from Shot A to Take 1 and then back to Shot A and then Take 2 without the audience realizing. This would work if you filmed the same thing with more than one camera or in more than one take.

From these examples, you can see that cutaways aren't just for making the edit look better; they're also great for making the point clearer. Cutaways can add to and enhance the story you're telling and keep people interested by showing what's being said from different points of view. The way to use a cutaway is pretty simple: you just put one clip on top of another to hide it completely.

When you choose Cutaway in iMovie for iOS and iPadOS, that's the only thing you can do with them. There is no greater choice of settings after that. There are, however, more settings in the Video overlay settings menu of iMovie for macOS that make it much more useful.

Adding fade transitions to overlays

In iMovie for macOS, you can fade in overlays. This way, you can add overlay clips slowly instead of having a split show up all at once. You can add them in two ways.

To begin, you can do the following:

1. Select the overlay and click the **Video overlay settings** button on the toolbar.
2. Click in the **duration editor** box and set a time for the fade in and fade out, accurate to 1/10 of a second:

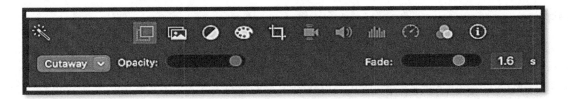

If you'd rather, you can click and drag the fade handles at the top of the timeline overlay. It's easier, faster, and can be changed in more ways.

You can drag the fade handles to exact frames if you zoom in on the timeline:

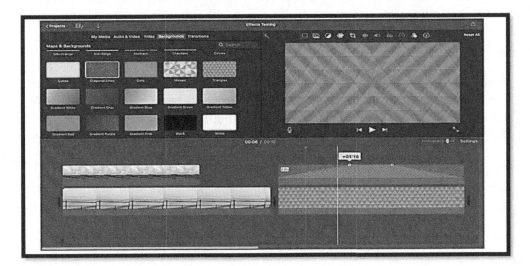

You can also change the length of the fade in and out by using the fade handles. On an overlay, every fade-in and fade-out lasts the same amount of time. These changes will make it harder to be creative with fade transitions because the fade-out has to make sense in the video too. Luckily, though, you can change the lengths of the fade-in and fade-out separately.

Here's how to change the length of just one fade:

- ○ Hold down the option key.
- ○ Click and drag the fade bar to the left or right.

The option key

In iMovie, the option key ⌥ extends your artistic options by letting you make small, precise changes that make editing easy. This Option key in macOS changes the way some choices look and how some tasks work. As time goes on and more actions are added to iMovie, mixing tools and actions with ⌥ may help you find even more ways to make it your own. So go for it! To make cutaways, use fade transitions like that. But fading in overlays can do more than just bring clips together easily. It can also give you a short double-exposure effect where you can see two clips at once, like in a cross-dissolve transition. We will now look at the other option in the Video overlay settings menu, which will make that happen permanently.

Creating Opacity effects

As soon as the split starts to fade in, it will cover up the main video layer unless you change the brightness of that layer. In iMovie for macOS, here's how to do that:

- ○ Pick out the media you want to use as an overlay in the Media Browser.
- ○ Press **Q** or drag it on top of a clip in the timeline.
- ○ On the menu, click the button that says "**Video overlay settings**." It will already be set to Cutaway style for the overlay.
- ○ Move the **Opacity too**l to the left to see more of the clip below.

So, lowering the density can make a double exposure effect last longer, but why would you want to? Won't it just make a mess of clips that don't do anything? Not all the time. People who watch movies and TV shows often think that two clips are connected in some way when they see double exposure. In this case, it could mean that:

- • Characters are dependent on one another
- • The character or subject wants a particular object or is thinking about it
- • Two different places or objects relate to each other or are both relevant to the story

However, these ways of using double exposure work best in story stories. You can still add value in other ways as well. A picture, like a map, could be added to a true clip to give it more background. I used an adjustable old-world map and a picture of a ship at sea to give the picture below some background for a made-up vacation trip to the United States. When I lower the brightness, the dark blue sea shows through the map clip, which is the overlay.

This type of photography works best when there is a lot of contrast between the dark and light parts of the picture. If the color parts are pretty much the same, the dark area will go away first and all at once when you lower the brightness. This lets you put other pictures on top of the bright parts of the first picture and add words in a different color. Like any other editing tool, double-exposure effects should only be used in small amounts. The effect will not be as interesting if there are too many double shots. It will look cheap. That's all we have to say about some artsy uses of invisibility. Aside from that, though, obscurity can also be useful. We're going to look at one that can make it a lot easier to edit projects with more than one camera view.

Multi-camera editing with cutaways and opacity effects

Using overlays and opacity edits with multiple cameras is much simpler, which is a real benefit. When you edit with more than one camera, you combine two shots of the same thing that were taken at the same time. Five or more cameras are used to film most TV shows, especially live ones. Live events are often recorded from different views so that the director can pick out the best parts from each camera later. We're going to look at this second way that multi-camera sets can be used: for editing. Maybe you can guess that if you put the closeup camera file after the wide camera file in the timeline and cut out the best parts, you'd end up with clips that are out of order and don't match the background audio. We need to edit the images from all of the cameras at the same time, which means we need to use overlays.

First, we need to add everything to the schedule:

1. Get the video and audio of the band playing.
2. Create a new iMovie project with the video and audio. The audio of the show, the wide camera footage, and the close-up camera footage should all make up three clips.
3. In the schedule, put the camera angle that you think you'll use most first.

I think you should add the close-up view first. As a backup in case the more interesting close-up angle gets out of focus or needs to be changed, the wide angle is there.

107

4. Put the background audio track at the bottom of the timeline and the other shot on top:

Our next job is to make sure that the two camera angles are synced with one another, as well as with the audio of the band performance.

Syncing multi-camera footage

When we edit video from more than one camera, we need to make sure that the shots are all in sync with each other. This way, when we switch from one shot to the next, the sound and screen moves will still match up. People will find it harder to watch, understand, and enjoy your video if they can tell the difference between them. To get things to sync, all you need is a short, loud sound and a picture that goes with it. If you remember, clap in front of the camera right after you press record. So, you can match up the sound of the clap with the sight of two hands coming together. The wide lens on this edit shows a band member dancing to the beat of the drums, which is a great example of how to sync.

Let's not worry about the main video layer right now and just sync the wide angle:

1. Start the **timeline (L)** and find the point where the guitarist starts to clap above their head.
2. Now we need to find the exact spot where the guitarist's hands touch. Use the ← and → button keys to move through the videos and look for where the hands first meet.
3. Move your mouse over the top clip and press **C** to pick it. Then, press M to add a note where the hands meet.
4. Use steps 2 through 3 again to mark the second and third claps. This will help the sync be more accurate.

5. Now pick the audio track and listen while also viewing the waveform. There are a lot of claps after the musician tells people to clap their hands. Each one makes a small peak in the sound. As shown below, use the letter M to mark the first, second, and third points;

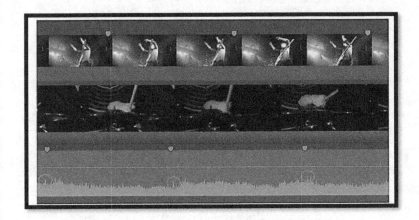

6. Now we need to get the two clips to work together. The audio clip should be moved to the right so that the sets of marks snap together. If they don't, press **N** to turn on snapping. Even if some don't line up perfectly, you should be able to draw a straight line through all of them. If you can't, make some small changes and watch the clip again until the drum beats and claps sound good together.

Now the audio and wide angle is in sync, but we still need to sync the close-up view. As a result, we will need to find another visual sign since the clapping can't be seen from this close-up position. It can be hard to sync up footage, which is why it's so important to plan, like remembering to clap at the beginning of a recording.

To line up the close-up shot, we'll look at the guitar in the close-up:

1. First, click on the top clip. Then, in the Video overlay settings menu, move the Opacity tool to the left to hide the clip. The close-up view will now show up when you move the playhead along the timeline.
2. The guitar will start to play after the first few drum beats of the song. The strings on a guitar need to be moved by the fingers and thumbs to be played. We can sync this clip now that we know that.
3. The thumb in the shot bends to hold the leftmost string just as the close-up camera moves away from the guitar. After that, put a mark (M) there. Remember that the arrow keys (← and →) give you more power over how the playhead moves:

4. Now that we've marked the video and audio beginnings of the guitar play, let's do the same thing with the video. Watch out for the first guitar sound as you play the timeline before the marking. It comes in after six drum beats to help. Put an M on the peak where the guitar playing begins:

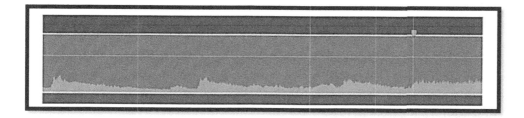

- Finally, it's time to make sure everything works right. Shift the background sound to the right so that the first audio tag lines up with the one we put on the close-up shot.
- So, move the top clip to the right so that its clapping markers line up with the three clapping markers later in the audio, as shown in the picture below. This will throw the wide angle out of sync again.

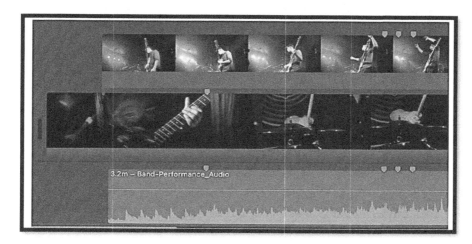

It doesn't matter if it seems hard; what you just did is about as hard as cutting clips together can get. If this doesn't work for you, here's a quick fix to get the videos to match up for this exercise:

1. Cut **2.8 seconds** off the beginning of the close-up shot.
2. Cut **0.3 seconds** off the beginning of the wide view.
3. The audio should be moved as far to the left as possible.

If you used marks to time the clips, you'll need to cut out the same parts so that there is no space in the video before the audio starts. We can now talk about the creative side of editing with more than one camera.

Editing multi-camera footage

We made the top layer (the wide angle) less opaque while we were combining footage in the last part so that we could see the closeup angle without having to move clips out of the way. We also didn't split or change the clip on the main video layer, and we didn't take any footage out. This means that all the footage is still in sync and saved on the timeline in case we need to make changes later. We picked a favorite camera angle when we added the clips to the timeline. This is because the shot on the main video layer will be the one you see the most when the other angle's opacity is set to 0%. When working with more than one camera in iMovie, the best way **to use opacity is to pick one shot as the priority and raise the opacity on the other shot when the first shot can't be used. That's easy to do:**

1. If the angle you want doesn't look good (for me, this meant the image wasn't clear or the video was too shaky), press C to pick the overlay and then D+B to make two splits around that area.
2. In **Video overlay settings**, drag its opacity to the right:

3. When you watch the video, the film will cut to the overlay for just the right amount of time.
4. Go to the next spot where the angle you want doesn't work and do steps 1 through 2.

It is much easier to edit video from more than one camera than to sync it in the first place. Now, as an editor, the most important thing is to use your best sense to choose where to stay on the right angle and where to cut to the other angle. **Besides cutting out parts of the desired angle that don't look good, you may also want to:**

- To refocus the audience (showing the whole room every once in a while, makes the video feel more logical).
- To show how everyone in the room talks to each other (for example, the main singer might wave to the guitar player, so you'll need to see both of them).

We all know that iMovie only lets you have one main video and one layer of related video, so there has to be a way to edit footage that has three or more shots happening at the same time. There should be at least three shots. Begin editing with the two you thinks you'll use most. We'll talk about adding the third angle later. That's all we have to say about multi-camera editing for now. Now we'll look at the other types of overlays that you can use in both sorts of iMovie.

Split screen and blue/green screen effects

Now we'll look at some of the other ways that iMovie lets you show overlays. There is a drop-down menu for video overlay settings. Split Screen is a simple but useful overlay style. The overlay clip is put next to the clip in the main video layer when Split Screen mode is used. Using split-screen clips is helpful when you want to make it look like two things are happening at the same time or next to each other. It's a great way to connect shots that were taken at different times and places; it makes it seem like they should be right next to each other. You could even use Split Screen to show two different views of the same person. For example, game shows will sometimes show a shot of a contestant's face and their fingers on a buzzer in this way. **To make a split screen effect on iOS or iPadOS and change how it looks:**

1. Put the clip you want to split screen on top of another clip in the timeline. To do this, tap the three dots and choose Add as... | Split Screen.
2. Tap the **zoom controls**, which are shown in the picture below as a magnifying glass in the upper right corner of the Viewer. The overlay picture will be on the right by default. You can zoom in or out by pinching:

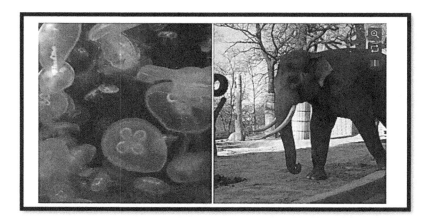

3. To change the other clip's view, tap the main video clip on the timeline and then tap the **zoom controls** again. The clip will take up the whole Viewer until you're done making changes and press the **zoom controls** again.
4. The **Viewer** has a button for rotating that is below the zoom tools. If you tap, the split screen layout will turn around 90 degrees. With two or three taps, the split between the clips changes from vertical to horizontal.
5. In Split Screen mode, the bottom button lets you add or remove a white line between the clips:

If you want to make the visual split between the clips more noticeable within the program, use the border, which is only available in the mobile version of iMovie. **Now, here's how to make iMovie for macOS have split-screen effects:**
1. Pick out a clip in the Media Browser that you want to split into two parts.
2. Press **Q** or drag it on top of a clip in the timeline.
3. Click on the box that says "**Video overlay settings**."
4. From the drop-down option of overlay styles, pick **Split Screen**.
5. With the **Position** drop-down button, you can change where the overlay appears on the screen. The overlay clip is where that menu says it is (top, bottom, right, left):

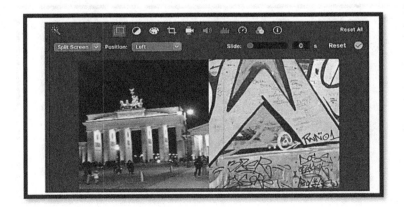

By moving one clip over the other when using Split Screen on a Mac, you can also transition into the split screen effect. The overlay clip slides in from the side of the frame given in the Position menu until it takes up half of the screen. This movement is called Slide. It's like the slide/wipe transition, but this one stops in the middle of the frame. The timeline doesn't have a fade handle that you can use to change the Slide transition as it does with fade transitions. **To change the time of the transition:**

1. Go to the **Overlay settings**.
2. In the duration editor box, type in the amount of time you want the transition to last.
3. Press "**Enter**" to keep the change.

The time you enter will show how long it takes for the slide-over motion to finish from the beginning of the overlay clip. At the end of the clip, the transition will go the other way, and the overlay will slide back out of the frame. One bad thing about the split screen effect is that you can't control the in and out movements separately. That's overlays for a split screen. It's not a big deal; it's just a simple effect that can make your projects look better when sharing another clip at the same time would give the video more contexts. Let's look at something bigger now.

Using Green/Blue Screen effects

Chroma keying is the process of cutting out parts of the screen based on their color. The Green/Blue Screen overlay style lets you do this. You can use this method to put yourself on top of a different background (this is what you might think of when you hear the term "green screening") or to cut out a form from the frame so you can see the clip below. In a strange twist, iMovie for iOS and iPadOS's chroma keying tool is a lot more advanced than most. It lets you key out any color you want based on where you tap. **That's what you do:**

1. Put a clip with a green or blue block on top of another clip (tap the **three dots** and choose **"Add as..."** then "**Green/Blue Screen**").
2. Most of the time, the effect will be performed naturally. To get rid of the effect, tap **Reset** in the upper left corner of the Viewer.
3. Click on the color inside the box that you want to get rid of. It's best to use the "**Tap to remove color**" effect on blue and green parts of the frame, but you can tap on any color to make it see-through as long as it's bright and stays the same:

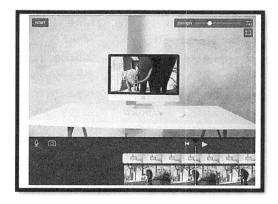

4. Using the Strength tool (top right of the picture), you can modify the keying's strength.
5. You can tap on the main video layer and change the zoom with zoom settings, just like with the split-screen effect. This changes what we see in the green screen area.

We are going to learn how to use this effect on macOS now. Different versions of iMovie have a few different blue and green screen options. You can only key out green and blue colors in iMovie for macOS, and you can't click on a color to make it see-through. The effect is made to happen automatically based on whether the frame is mostly green or blue. **To make a blue/green screen effect on a Mac:**

1. Pick the clip you want to change to blue or green and drag it on top of another clip (or press **Q**).
2. Click on the box that says "**Video overlay settings**."
3. From the drop-down box, pick **Green or Blue Screen**.

I used the Green/Blue Screen effect on a clip where a blue circle grows on a green background to make the picture below. My **Aquarium-vid-2** can be seen when I key out the background. Mac users should know that where you put the playhead is important. The effect I used was at the very end of the clip, where iMovie keyed out the green color (since most of the frame was still green). **It tried to key out the blue any further, but that didn't work well because the circle has more than one shade of blue:**

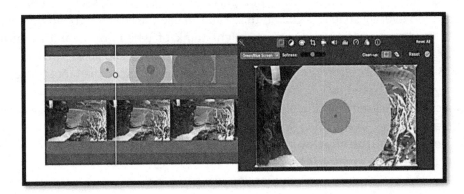

4. Using the **Softness slider** next to the drop-down option, you can change how hard you press the keys.
5. You can change how the clip in the main video layer is framed by using the **Crop menu** in the toolbar and moving the **Crop to fill** box.

Crop is an option in both versions of iMovie. In the picture above, it is chosen under Clean-up. You can screen out parts of the clip by removing whole parts of the overlay that you don't want to keep. This tool is pretty limiting, though, since you can only drag four places. You can only mask out blocky parts of the screen with this, so it wouldn't help if you wanted to hide, say, the shape of someone's head. The Eraser tool is also in the **Clean-up** menu. If you click on any green or blue spots that are still visible, you can erase them. This is kind of like the "**Tap to remove color**" option on the mobile version, but you can't use it the same way because the blue/green screen effect is always already there. iMovie looks for the closest green or blue in the frame even if there isn't any. Often, it finds something bad. The eraser tool is better for getting rid of small bits of blue or green that haven't been fully keyed out. That's all there is to the **Green/Blue Screen** tool. We will now look at the last type of overlay, which includes the whole overlay clip in the main video.

Using Picture-in-Picture effects in iMovie

Picture in Picture (PiP) is one of the most flexible effects in iMovie. It lets you change the size of the overlay clip so that it fits inside the main video frame. As we'll see later, you can also move the clip around the frame as the video plays. PiP is a great way to show extra information that doesn't fit into a split. PiP isn't the most subtle of effects, but it can give your video a lot more meaning. How to add a PiP.

For iOS and iPadOS:

- Tap the **three dots** and choose **Add as... | Picture in Picture** to put the clip you want to show inside the frame of another clip.
- Inside the main video, the clip will show up as a smaller of itself:

With the options in the upper right corner of the Viewer, you can now change how the PiP looks. These are them from top to bottom:

- Tap the **zoom buttons** (the icon that looks like a magnifying glass), then pinch the picture to move it in and out of the PiP.
- To move the PiP, tap the compass points and pull it. To change its size, pinch in and out.
- To get rid of the edge that is usually put around the PiP, toggle the option at the bottom. If you want the PiP to fit in with the image or if its background is see-through, you should get rid of the border. If you don't, the border will look like a weird picture frame.

In the mobile version of iMovie, those steps are pretty much all you can do with PiP. However, iMovie for macOS has more customization options. To add a PiP, do it this way:

- Drag the file you want to use as a PiP on top of another one, or press Q.

- From the drop-down menu that appears, click the Video overlay settings button on the toolbar and pick Picture in Picture.

You can change more about the edge in the Video overlay settings section than in the mobile app:

1. You can adjust the border to one of three settings using the Border option.

- No border
- Thin border
- Thick border

2. There is an option next to the **Border selection** that will open the macOS Colors wheel so you can pick a color for the border.

3. If you check the box next to **Shadow** to the right of the screen, the picture will have a drop shadow that makes it stand out even more. But the shadow is pretty straight and blocky, so it's probably only worth using if the PiP would be hard for people to see on the screen:

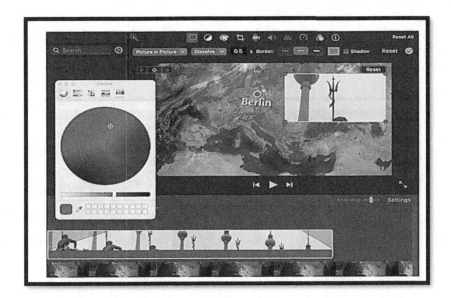

When the sample PiP in the picture above fades in, it uses the timeline's fade handles. However, on macOS, PiP overlays can use different transition styles. Let us look at those.

Using Zoom and Swap transitions with PiP

When you use overlays, dissolve is the most likely transition to be used because it lets you slowly add an overlay using the fade handles on the timeline. However, when adding transitions to PiP, we have the option to be a little crazier if the mood of the video calls for it by choosing the Zoom or Swap animation style. Let's start with Zoom. The PiP and its border don't fade in as a whole picture; instead, the motion makes them grow from the part that is closest to the edge of the screen.

We can change the transition by:

- In the Video overlay settings menu, click on the second drop-down menu and pick Zoom.
- With the time designer box, you can change how long the zoom will last.
- To save your changes, press "**Enter**":

For some reason, you can't change the length of a zoom transition on the timeline. Fade handles only show up and work for Dissolve transitions. This means that there will always be a zoom-out motion of the same length that you can't change. This is the same as with Slide for split-screen effects. Having this in the video restricts your artistic options with Zoom, which is why transitions are generally better. The last transition style isn't quite the same. You can change which clip is shown in the PiP with swap without moving anything in the sequence. In the period editing menu, you can set how long the main picture should be shown. This keeps it in the PiP box for the amount of time you choose. **To get this going:**

1. In the **Video overlay settings** menu, click on the second drop-down menu and select **Swap**.
2. Change the length of the zoom animation with the **duration editor** box.
3. To save your changes, press "**Enter**":

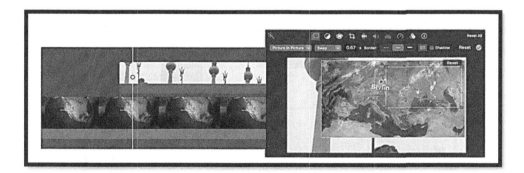

It's possible to see why this transition is named Swap: the clip on top of the overlay becomes the one that fills the whole frame, while the clip in the main video layer acts as a point of view (PiP). While swapping can be very artistic, it can also be hard to understand when the clips switch roles.

It might help to mark the clips (**M**) so that you can see when they're switched. The **Zoom and Swap transitions** can work well for styled movies, but the **Dissolve transitions** with fade handles are still the most flexible way to set up overlays. They can cut right away like a split or slowly add clips like a normal cross-dissolve transition. We can also control the fade-in and fade-out transitions separately. It is also important to note that the keyframe tool can only be used with the dissolve transition type. **Using keyframe animations on macOS** The keyframe editor is a powerful drawing tool that can only be used on macOS. But let's talk about what a keyframe is first so we know what we're talking about. Another word for a keyframe is a save point. If you set a keyframe for an object at 00:03 and then move it again at 00:08, you can always play it back at 00:03 because that's where the keyframe was set. **A keyframe saves a motion state that can't be changed:**

The moving object (in iMovie, this can be a PiP clip or an audio level) goes as easily as possible from the first keyframe to the second. So, you can make a motion path by setting more than one keyframe. But we're not talking about hand-drawn cartoons. Instead, think of a character model jumping around the frame to look like a person who isn't there. **So, let's look at how to use keyframes to animate a PiP:**

- Change the style of the overlay to "**Picture in Picture**" and add a clip as an overlay (Q).
- Find a spot near the beginning of the overlay clip or where you want the PiP to begin moving.
- Click and drag the PiP in the Viewer to choose where you want to start.
- In the **keyframe editor**, click the **middle button** to add a new keyframe at the playhead.
- There will be a cross in the diamond in the middle of the keyframe editing area. This means that a keyframe has been set where the playhead is:

Creative choices for PiP animations

You should only set two keyframes: one at the beginning and one at the end of the clip. This will make your PiP move in a smooth step. Like a Ken Burns effect, the PiP will move in a smooth line that way. Adding more keyframes across the clip will give it a more realistic, shaky look. Be aware, though, that setting numerous keyframes closely together and allowing for a lot of movement between them will make the animation appear jumbled. Try to keep keyframes about the same distance apart at all times so the PiP doesn't jump around a lot. Also, try not to change the size of the PiP because the overlay will look weird when it changes size while moving. Of course, it's okay to do either of these things if you have a creative reason for them or a reason in your story for them to happen. It's about making sure that the people watching can understand and agree with what you're doing.

- Move the playhead to the spot on the timeline where you want to start the next track.
- To put the second keyframe where the playhead is, click the middle button of the **Keyframe editor** area again.
- The left and right button keys in the Keyframe editing area let you move between the keyframes you've set.
- When you're on a keyframe, the square and the x icon in the middle will both show-up. To get rid of that clip, click the middle button again.

It's important to remember that you can still change the cutting style and add Ken Burns effects to the picture itself while the overlay is moving across the screen. Do these things:

- There is an overlay clip in the sequence. Click on it.
- Click the **Crop** button on the toolbar.
- You can switch between **Ken Burns** and **Crop to fill** styles whenever you want. Then, pick **Crop to fill** and move the crop box around to see the whole picture.

When you drag the crop box to fill the whole frame (but don't use the Fit style), the black bars next to the clip become clear and won't show up in the PiP. This is where Crop to Fill comes in handy. You can animate any PiP with the keyframe editor, but the effect works best on small pictures with no background. It won't look as interesting and unique to animate a square 16:9 frame around a bigger 16:9 frame as it would with a more organic shape. That's all we have to say about PiP cartoons. But you can create a lot more in iMovie with keyframes.

Using audio keyframes

Moving a visible thing isn't always what animation means. Over time, something can change into a motion. The same is true for audio levels. When you edit audio in iMovie, you may remember that the volume is shown as a line. The volume level line for a clip will go up or down and stay straight if you change the volume of that clip. But with keyframes, you can move that audio line along a path, changing the volume of the sound as you please. Audiences will enjoy audio transitions that are as smooth as the shapes on the timeline. **To make keyframes for audio on a Mac:**

- Click on the audio level line and ***Option Key + click*."

- A keyframe for the audio will be made, which is shown on the timeline as a dot. The volume for your audio animation starts with this first keyframe.
- To add another audio keyframe further along the clip, press the **Option Key and click**. This is where you want the volume motion to happen.
- You can move the second keyframe up or down by clicking and dragging it.
- Pay attention to the audio. As the audio gets louder or softer, you should hear:

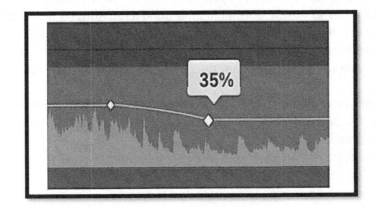

- If you click and drag an audio keyframe along the timeline, you can move it. The sound changes more slowly when there is more time between keyframes.
- You're likely too close to the last keyframe if you can't place this one. Press the **Option Key and click** again after moving the playhead a little.
- To get rid of a keyframe, right-click on it and choose "**delete keyframe**."

You can gently fade sound when you're not at the end of a clip and can't use the fade handles. You can make and use audio keyframes instead. You can also make your fades that fit any shape you want because you can make as many keyframes as you want. This is helpful if you want to cut audio from an interview where the person you're filming says something interesting and then quickly starts a new line that you don't need. A good way to stop the next line without making it sound like you cut the speaker off too abruptly is to make a fade curve like the one below:

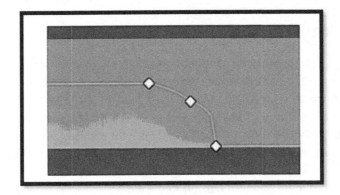

There are countless ways that audio keyframes can be helpful, but I'll list one more: using a range (R) to separate and get rid of annoying sounds:

1. Find the sound's shape. Knocks and other sounds you don't want are often made up of short, sharp peaks.
2. Hold down **R and click** and drag over the audio clip to make a range around the waveform that is as small as possible so that it fits the sound.
3. Move the sound level line inside the area to 0%. Two keyframes on either side of the area will keep the level of the rest of the clip the same:

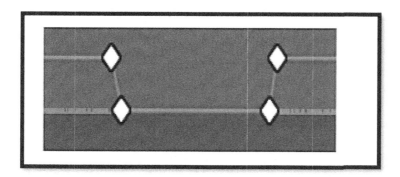

4. To fill the gap you made, copy some room tone, which is background noise, from somewhere else. When it drops to 0%, the audio will have a shocking stutter:

If you can, make sure that the room tone you copy doesn't have any voices or other sounds that you can recognize. It will be clear that you copied audio from somewhere else if it does because the sound will play over and over again.

5. After listening to the audio again, if you can't tell that it was edited, you did it right!

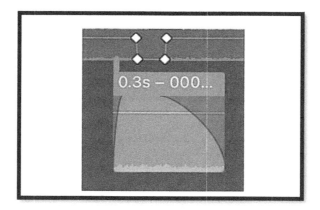

While the picture above shows an edit that was done to audio that was part of a video clip, the process is the same for audio that is in its clips. This was one way to make a change happen slowly. Next, we'll look at how to use transitions to make visual changes happen slowly.

Using transition effects – speed and color ramping

If you change the color information, the clip will look very different, which is not good for keeping people interested. Changes that happen slowly keep the audience interested in the story and let you change how you tell it subtly. Individual clips can be used as keyframes in iMovie, and **cross-dissolve** transitions between them can be used to make slow and steady changes in speed and color (an effect known as ramping). This can be done with iMovie's built-in color effects by going to **Modify > Fade to**. We can do more with the effect if we edit it by hand, though. Ramping works for changing color, clip filters, and speed, which are all menu options.

On macOS, here's how to make any of those effects stronger:

1. To add the effect, split the clip you want to use (Command + B) and move the playhead as close to the middle as you can:

To make their movements, transitions use the same amount of the first and second clips. For example, a 3-second transition would use 1.5 seconds of each.

2. During the transition to the second clip, change the speed or color as needed.
3. To connect the two clips, press Command + T and add a cross-dissolve transition.
4. Keep an eye on the transition. Change the length of the transition by double-clicking on it, typing in a new number, and pressing Enter. This will make the change happen more slowly, or maybe not at all.

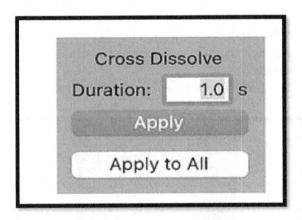

That being said, why might you want to add effects slowly? All of this helps keep the viewers' attention on what they're watching. Effects that are introduced without being seen can be useful in two situations where you don't want the effect to be seen:

- Adding a color change to change the mood of a scene slightly (for example, dropping the color temperature to make it sadder).
- Increasing the speed of a clip to fit it into a shorter time limit. The more slow the change in speed, the less likely it is that people will notice it.

Keep in mind, though, that this method doesn't work with clips that move shakily or Ken Burns cartoons because the transition doesn't happen right away. It's possible to see the two clips in different places at the same time during the transition if there is a lot of movement. This is called double exposure, and it's not the effect you want. That breaks the atmosphere, which is a shame. Also, you might not want to use these effects if you are adding a part that is sped up a lot, like a timelapse. Cutting to a color or filter change can also be just the right kind of shocking to get people to pay attention when you're making a video and want to show how different the clips are. You don't have to do anything wrong when you edit; you just need to do things for a reason. We will now go back to the problems with one layer of related media and find a classic way to get around them.

Combining effects – creating compound clips

The fact that iMovie only allows for one linked video layer is a limitation that often presents itself as a barrier, regardless of whether you are attempting to edit footage from three cameras or desire several PiPs. The good news is that there is a straightforward solution to this problem, although not the best one: combining two clips into a single compound clip. **Although it is a rather straightforward procedure, there are a few things that can be of assistance:**

- A new project dedicated to your compound clip
- Plenty of space on your hard drive, or external storage space
- Some time and patience for exporting and reimporting clips

Creating compound clips in iMovie revolves around a few simple steps:

- ○ Carry out a fine cut using two video layers, making certain that everything is to your satisfaction on both sides.
- ○ Create a master copy of the edited version of the file.
- ○ Import the master copy again, which is now a single layer, and then create a new layer as linked media on top of it.

The problem is that we can't edit the original clips since we're exporting and importing clips. For this reason, it is recommended that you maintain the distinct components of your compound clip in a project that is unique to itself. In this manner, you can make edits and export the compound clip once again if you re-import your combined effect and then discover that something isn't quite right. There is nothing about the process of producing compound clips in iMovie that should be difficult; it is just incredibly repetitive and takes a significant amount of time to do. Because of this, you should truly question yourself if you need to add more visual layers on top of your project since it is necessary. In addition to the possibility of your frame being cluttered, it is going to be a major time waste, particularly if you do not have a strategy for where to stop. Your creative constraint should be the only restriction on how many PiPs you can add to your effects or shots to your multi-camera edit. Remember that you should never build an edit simply to do an edit. Because you can export and reimport over and over again indefinitely, the only limit you should have is your creative potential. Let's have a look at the process of making compound clips, shall we? After doing a search on Pexels for the term "Gig crowd," I came across a realistic photograph of a crowd that was titled "**Video of People Having Fun at Concert.**" Check to see if you can locate anything comparable to what you are doing if you are following along; use your creative muscles!

Let us go via the steps that are listed below:

To prevent the loss of quality that may occur as a result of exporting and re-importing several times, you are required to export using the highest quality settings that are available.

- If there is a video of a crowd that you would want to utilize, try downloading it.
- Create a new project by pressing the **Command and N** keys simultaneously on the **iMovie Projects screen (2).**
- Include the audience footage as well as the compound clip that you have created of the performance in your presentation.
- You should begin by adding the compound clip to the timeline (W), and then proceed to add the crowd shot as an overlay (Q).
- Select the **Video overlay** settings option, and then move the Opacity slider to the left side of the screen. The following is the method that we had previously used to see through to the primary perspective of the performance:

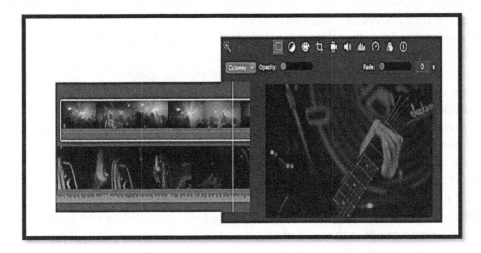

As a result of the fact that the shot of the crowd is not synchronized with the performance (and is significantly shorter), we are going to select the most appropriate locations to cut to the crowd. This includes any instances in which there is nothing, in particular, happening during the **performance, as well as any areas that you may have missed in the past where the camera is moving between shots or out of focus:**

- Divide the footage of the crowd into many clips, each for around three seconds. These are going to be distributed throughout the performance.
- In the area where you want to transition to a clip of the crowd, move the short segment of the crowd clip to the correct spot, and then drag the Opacity slider back to the right. Having done so, you have successfully generated a typical cutaway for the audience.

If at all possible, try to cut to the audience and then away from it while you are in the midst of a sentence. Because of this, the cut itself becomes less noticeable, which is exactly what we want when we are trying to create a continuous video of the band's performance.

- When you are satisfied that you have included all of the cutaways to the audience that you want, export a master copy.

Using compound clips in iMovie requires us to rinse and redo the regular editing process until we have added all of the additional angles or clips that we need. This describes the nature of the process. Indeed, this solution is not very beautiful; nevertheless, because there is no official compound clip function (or more video layers to deal with), it is necessary to make the most of what you have available to you. In the end, creative problem-solving is going to increase your editing skills and make you a better editor. What about doing this with iMovie for iOS and iPadOS? That is one option to consider. There is no reason why this method of creating compound clips should not work with the mobile app for iMovie, but you should be aware that what is a labor of love on a Mac can rapidly become a labor of love on an iPhone or iPad. When editing, using a keyboard makes the editing process far quicker and more effective. Having to deal with touch activities is likely to significantly lengthen the duration of this procedure; nevertheless, it is possible that this may not necessarily be a negative thing. Let the amount of time that I have to spend be a factor that I take into consideration: do I need this edit for my video to properly convey its story? Most of the time, the most basic editing does the best.

CHAPTER 13

INTEGRATING KEYNOTE – TITLES AND ANIMATIONS

Creating custom titles with Keynote

If you want to create personalized titles, the first thing you need to do is create a dedicated Keynote file that you can return to throughout the process. When you want to generate titles **for your projects, you won't have to go through the same initial stages again since this does not need you to do so:**

1. Launch Keynote by either double-clicking on the program icon or searching for it using Spotlight after pressing the Command Key and the spacebar.
2. You may either use the shortcut Command Key + N or click the New Document button.
3. You will be presented with the theme chooser at this point.

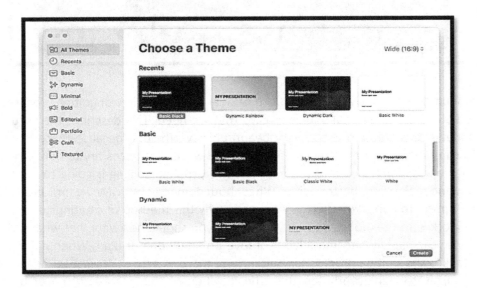

To create titles that include alpha channels, we want the presentation to be as straightforward as possible. Click the Create button once you have selected the Basic Black format.

4. The primary menu for altering slides will now be shown to you. Select the background of the slide by clicking on it. If you have completed this step, you will see that the **Format sidebar** on the right-hand side will have the Slide header, as shown in the figure below.

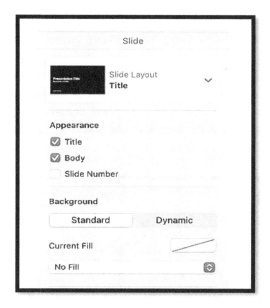

5. Look at the sidebar at the bottom of the page to find the option that says **Current Fill**. It is this option that determines the color of the slide's back, so make sure you choose it. To get an alpha channel, we must ensure that there is no color present, thus we will pick **"No Fill"** from the drop-down selection.
6. The removal of the unneeded text boxes may be accomplished by clicking on them and then using the backspace key. This step is dependent on the kind of title that you want to make.

To keep just the main title untouched for customization, I prefer to get rid of the **Presentation Subtitle** as well as the **Author and Date** boxes.

7. Double-click on **Presentation Title**, and then write the words you wish to appear in the title. To select all of the text, do a **triple click** or use the **Command Key + A**.

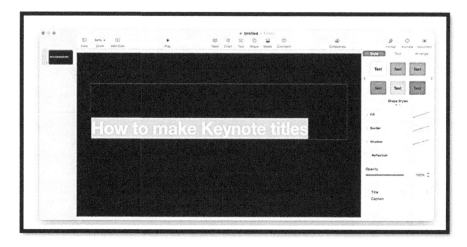

8. When you look at the sidebar for **Format** at this moment, you should see three tabs: **Style, Text, and Arrange**. When you click on **Text**, you may alter the font and color of the text.

9. You are free to make whatever modifications to the font that you choose; however, I strongly recommend that you give the font a drop shadow, which will help the font stand out from the background of your video. Simply click on the gear icon that is located below the point size indicator, and then choose the **Shadow option** from the hover menu that displays. This will allow you to create a drop shadow.

10. You now have a Keynote file that serves as an excellent basis for the creation of individualized titles thanks to your efforts. You should save the document by pressing the **Command Key and the S key,** and then choose a place and a name that are simple to recall before you proceed with the customization of this title.

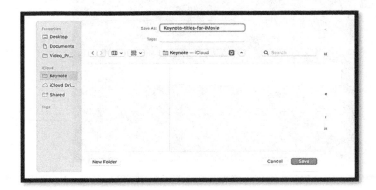

Maintaining your title documents in the iCloud folder that Keynote uses as its default save location is something that I would strongly recommend doing. As a result of the fact that Keynote files (.Key) are very short files that do not use a significant amount of storage space in iCloud, having them stored in your iCloud Drive enables you to view your title documents on any Apple device you possess, provided that you are connected to the internet via that device.

Exporting Keynote titles

Now that you have a suitable stock title that you can alter and reformat to suit your requirements, it is time to try exporting the title and importing it into iMovie. You can do this by following the steps stated in the previous sentence. Whether or whether your title is compatible **with iMovie is determined by the options that you choose from the export menu; thus, you must follow along to get some experience with your title:**

1. Once you have completed your title slide and are satisfied with it, click on the slide to double-check that the **Background** is set to **No Fill**.
2. To export images, go to the menu bar and choose **File**, then **Export to**, and finally **Images**. There is no shortcut on the keyboard for this.
3. You'll be shown the **Export Your Presentation** menu. Ensure that you are currently on the Images tab;

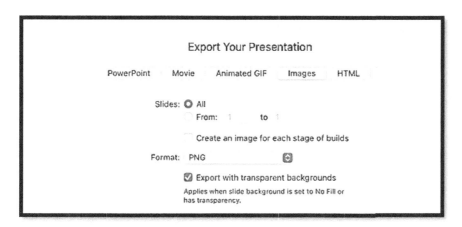

4. If you have more than one slide (often for various titles), click the **From** circle and alter the number in both boxes to represent the slide number you wish to export (for example, 1 to 1). This will allow several slides to be exported.
5. Ensure that the format is selected to either **PNG or TIFF** in the drop-down option, and if it is not already checked, make sure that the box that says "**Export with transparent backgrounds**" is checked.

Afterward, choose an acceptable location to store the title by clicking the Next... button located in the bottom right corner of the menu. If you create a folder in Finder that is specifically designated for videos, it would be a good idea to store the title picture in that folder.

Images and transparency

To ensure that they get a picture with a transparent background rather than a white background, some individuals use the PNG file format while searching for photographs that do not have a background. This is because transparency appears white in search engines. **Even while it is possible for pictures to include an alpha channel, the PNG format does not provide them with one.**

It is important to keep in mind the following:

> **.JPEG** files cannot carry transparency
> **.PNG**, **.HEIC**, and **.TIFF** files can carry transparency
.PNG is often the best choice because it has great compatibility but cleverly compresses images to give you small files compared to others.**TIFF**, which is a lossless image format.

Importing Keynote files into iMovie

The .PNG file that you have produced from Keynote can then be imported into iMovie once you have done so. These title graphics can be used as cutaways or PIP because of their translucent background. This is the ideal way to utilize title graphics in a PiP format since it allows for the greatest flexibility. This gives you the ability to enlarge the title such that the text fills the whole screen, as well as to move the title around according to keyframe animations. **Your title will appear in the timeline if you follow these steps:**

- o Launch iMovie and double-click on the project that you want to utilize the title in by using the mouse.
- o Navigate to the **Project Media tab** and then hit the shortcut button for the import. Press the Command Key and the letter I.
- o Once you have located the title picture, import it. While you are exporting from Keynote, it will be placed in a folder with the name that you provided, and the filename of the first title picture will have the number **.001** added to it. This will occur even if you did not export several photos.

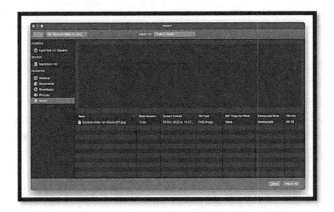

131

- Either choose a clip of your choosing or go to the **Backgrounds Media Browser** tab **(Command Key + 4).** The clip will serve as the background for the title. The clip should be added to the timeline.

In general, you should strive to make the background of the title as simple wherever possible. It will be necessary to use a drop shadow or text outline that is more robust to make the title legible if the background has a greater variety of colors and patterns.

- Return to the **Project Media** tab and add the picture of the title file as an overlay by pressing the Q key.
- Go to the toolbar, click the option labeled "**Video overlay settings**," and then use the drop-down menu to change the overlay style to "**PiP**." After that, choose the picture that will serve as the title.
- To have the title appear immediately, drag the fade handles to the edge of the clip on the timeline. This will cause the title to appear immediately. There is also the option of modifying the length of the transition to **zero** inside the **duration editor box**.
- To make the title bigger and ensure that it occupies the majority of the screen, click and drag the blue handles located in the corner of the PiP in an outward direction.

It is important to make sure that the point of view snaps against the yellow vertical and horizontal symmetry lines in the Viewer to create a visually appealing title. Even while it is not necessary to have a title that is symmetrical or that covers the screen, it is important to keep in mind that if you want to be unorthodox, there is a purpose for doing so: the audience will notice. That takes care of everything that pertains to Keynote's custom static titles. Make adjustments to the color and font of your text, as well as play about with the **Advanced Options (the gear symbol)** in Keynote to adjust the shadow weight, blur and opacity, character and line spacing, and other adjustments, to get the title that you want. Regardless of how you choose to create your static title, the process of exporting and importing it into iMovie will operate in the same manner. From this point forward, we are going to examine the process of animating titles, which necessitates a somewhat different export procedure to enable the animation to be recorded.

Creating animated titles in Keynote

Titles that ripple, fade, and grow into position are features of iMovie that you are acquainted with. This can also be accomplished using Keynote by utilizing the Build In, Action, and Build Out animations that it offers. You may be already acquainted with these sorts of animations from PowerPoint presentations: text that is dropping, speeding up, and whirling onto the screen. With the help of Keynote, we can apply these animations while still exporting just the title with an alpha channel. **To develop a title that introduces itself, the following steps should be taken:**

o   Let's begin by opening the Keynote file that you made for the iMovie titles.
o   In Keynote, go to the top right of the toolbar and click on the text box that surrounds your content. Then, click the **animate** button.

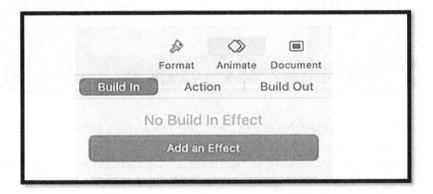

o   If the **Build In** section is not already highlighted, pick that tab to bring it into that position. You can add an effect by clicking on the button.
o   You have access to a vast array of special effects that can be applied to your title text. These effects are shown in distinct parts to accommodate a variety of motion scenarios. You can preview what the animation looks like by hovering over an effect and clicking the Preview button that is located to the right of it.
o   Once you have selected an effect, click on it, and a menu for modification will automatically appear in the sidebar of the animate window. Although the options will alter depending on the animation that you choose, **most of them will enable you to modify the following:**
- **Duration** of the animation
- **Direction** of the animation (from the left or the right)
- **Delivery** (allowing you to break up animations for larger bits of text, slow the start and end of animations, or add extra icons to the animation)
- **Order** (ignore this for now unless it's not 1

- Click the **Preview button** after you have finished fine-tuning the animation settings. This will allow you to confirm that the text displays in the manner that you like. If this is not the case, continue to make little adjustments and examine them until you are satisfied with the title animation.

Exporting animated titles from Keynote

When you are satisfied, it is time to start exporting. Because we are working on an animation that requires a significant amount of time to finish, we are unable to export the title as a picture. **Instead, we will need to export a Movie and then make adjustments to its settings to maintain the transparency of the slide.**

- To export to a movie, choose **File > Export To > Movie** from the menu bar.
- Verify that the slide range corresponds to what you desire (e.g., **3** to **3** if you're exporting one animated title of many), then save the file.
- At the bottom of the menu is the **Resolution** drop-down menu. Take a look at it, and then pick Custom...
- The list of available options expands. Make sure that the **Frame Rate** is the same as the one you are using for your project, and if necessary, alter it using the drop-down option.
- The **Compression Type** option is the one that has to be modified for us to export with an alpha channel. HEVC should be selected by clicking on that drop-down menu.
- The last option that is located underneath this menu will now be available for selection. If the **Export with transparent backgrounds** option is not already checked be sure you check it.

- Select the **Next** button, and then save the video file to the folder that contains your project.

Exporting transparency in video

In the past, we saw that.PNG and TIFF files both have transparency, however, TIFF files do not. Not at all, JPEG files. Within the realm of video, some formats essentially eliminate transparency. Both **HEVC** and **Apple ProRes 4444** are the two Compression-type options that are available in the Keynote export menu. Both of these options maintain transparency. Similar to the.**PNG file format**, the **High-Efficiency Video Coding (HEVC)** format generates smaller files while maintaining the majority of their quality and transparency. When you use **ProRes 4444**, you will get a file that is virtually entirely uncompressed and similar. The file is going to be quite large since it is a **TIFF** file. It's quite unlikely that you'll need the additional information that ProRes 4444 makes available. After you have generated your animated title from Keynote, the process of importing it into your timeline is quite similar to the approach that you would use for photos. However, it is important to keep in mind that throughout the process of adding your title clip to the timeline, you notice that the title does not begin its animation until around halfway through the clip. There is no need to be concerned about this; the reason for this is simply that we have not yet modified the build order settings for the animation system. That's something we're going to look at next.

Creating multi-stage animations with Build Order

Right now we have a title that builds in (shows up with an image). We'll add to this by making a second part of our title that moves with a different effect. **Okay, let's add another text box to our title slide and make it move:**
1. Open the title slide you were working on in Keynote.
2. Click once on the title text box, then press **Command Key + C and Command Key + V** to copy and paste it into the second text box. Make sure the text in both boxes has the same style settings.
3. Select all the words in the new text box by clicking three times and then type your new title.
4. Look for your second text box in the **Animate** tab and make sure the **Order** is set to **2**.

5. Click **Change** at the top of the **Animate** page and pick a new motion. I picked **Sparkle** to go with the writing.
6. Now it's time to connect these images. Click on the **Build Order** button at the very bottom of the **Animate** section.
7. Click on the second motion in the Build Order menu that appears and change the Start drop-down menu to **With Build 1.**

When these build events are used instead of click events, animations will now follow each other automatically instead of Keynote putting in pauses.

8. At the bottom of the screen, click Preview. Both text boxes should move at the same time.
9. **You can modify the following options to alter the animation's appearance:**
    o The duration of each transition
    o The delay in the second animation

Right now is your chance to take charge and change the settings to suit your artistic needs. Make small changes and then look at how they work. Then do it again. To show how the tools work, I'll show you what I'd change to make these images better. The Keyboard motion looks too fast when I preview it at 1.5 seconds—at least for how fast I type! It looks more like real typing, so I'm going to slow it down. To:

10. In the **Build Order** menu, click on the first animation. You can move the Duration tool in the Animate tab. Look ahead and judge: It takes **2.5 seconds**, which is about right.

Now I want the second title to appear when the first animation is almost done. To do that, we need a wait that's about the same length of time as the first transition.

11. In the **Build Order** menu, click on the second transition and edit the number in the Delay box. Preview and evaluate: a **1.8-second** pause works well.

Once you're pleased with your title, use the same export settings as before to turn it into a video. Keynote will use the delay we set between transitions instead of picking its delay now that we are using build order (**With Build 1**) instead of click events. In the **Build Order** box, click on the first animation and change **On Click** to **After Transition**. This will make the animation start as soon as the video does. That's it for now. We're going to add to our animation build order by animating the titles off the screen as well.

Building out animations

These are the images that go with our titles. Right now, they're just sitting there until the clip stops. We could just press the Option Key and click and drag the fade handle at the end of the clip on the timeline to make them fade out. But what if we want to move the titles out of view too?

1. Click on the first text box again.
2. Click on **Build Out** and then **Add an Effect** in the Animate tab.

You are now making a new motion for the same text box. The built-in animation is still there, though, so don't worry. In Keynote, you can give any object one Build In animation, one Action animation, and one Build Out animation. In the Build Order window, they will all be shown.

3. Click on a **Build Out** effect. Next, do steps 1–3 again for the second text box.

I chose Keyboard again as the **Build Out** motion for my first text box, which has the **Keyboard animation**. I changed the Keyboard animation's **Build Out Direction** to **Backward** in the **Animation** tab. This makes it look like the backspace key is getting rid of the words. I picked Vanish as the Build Out motion for the second text box, which has the Sparkle animation.

4. Click on the "**Build Order**" button. If you're following along, the menu should look like the picture below, but it depends on which movements you pick.

137

Now that all the steps are set up, we can use the Build Order menu to put them in the right order. First, we need to make sure that all of the movements happen on their own:

5. Right now, **Builds 3 and 4** are set to start on click, which we can tell because their logos are physically split from the other builds in the menu.
6. Click on **Build 3** and pick **After Build 2** from the menu that comes up.
7. Click on **Build 4** and pick **With Build 3** from the drop-down box that appears. Now the **Build Order** menu should look like the picture below.

It's also helpful to be able to see at a look what the builds are doing in Keynote. In the picture, you may notice that there are straight lines between some builds and partial dotted lines between others:

- If there is a dashed line between two builds, they happen at the same time.
- Two builds in a straight line mean they happen one after the other.

When you look at these lines, it's easier to see how your animations are connected. This makes it easier to find and change the right delays and actions when making more complicated animations. The next thing we need to do is set the delay for the Build Out movements. The title will stay on the screen for this amount of time before expanding, and both text boxes will expand at the same time.

8. Click on **Build 3** and fill in the **Delay** box with a time. To save the changes, press "**Enter.**"

What length of time you want your title to stay on screen is up to you. I chose a 2-second pause. You can check the motion to see if anything went wrong and decide what you want to change by looking at it first. I want the Vanish animation to end at the same time as the Keyboard animation, but I don't want them to start at the same time. One animation needs to have its start time pushed back, but its animation needs to take less time to finish. That way, the wait time plus the length of time is the same for both.

9. Go to the **Build Order** menu and click on **Build 4**. Then, add a 0.5-second pause. To save your changes, press "**Enter.**"
10. Press the **Build 3** button. **Edit Duration** in the **Animate** tab to make it 0.5 seconds longer than Build 4 (e.g., 2.5 seconds instead of 2 seconds).

When we play a preview of the animation, we can see that the time is right, but Vanish makes the word disappear into dust before the animation is over. This will be fixed by what I'm about to do:

11. Add one more second of delay to **Build 4 (Vanish)** so that the word **Sparkle** goes away when the **Keyboard** animation is over.

Exporting, importing, and adjusting multi-stage animations

We'll use some timeline tricks to make it easier to bring in a new title clip since we've already exported an animated one:

1. Click on File, and then Export To, then Movie.
2. Make sure that the codec is still HEVC and that the box next to Export with clear backgrounds is checked.
3. Click "**Next**," then save the video file to your project folder.
4. In iMovie, navigate to the appropriate project and press Command Key + I to import the file.
5. Copy the old title clip (**Command Key + C**) before you add the new title video to the timeline.
6. Choose the new clip in the Media Browser, then click and drag it on top of the old one to erase it.
7. Pick out the new clip and press **Alt+Command+U** to copy the overlay settings from the old clip to it. So, you don't have to make the same PiP changes again.

Also, we can change the style of the title without having to reorganize the Build Order menu now that we've made the sound for it. If you choose to change the color of the titles or move the shadows around after importing the title video into iMovie, you can do so without having to change or re-edit the animations. **I went back into Keynote and used the Format tab to make the following changes to the picture above:**

- I used the Text Color drop-down box to give all the words a color fill except Keynote, which got a yellow-to-blue gradient fill.
- For Sparkle, I made a picture filled with polka dots.
- I used the gear menu to move the shadows to the bottom of the words and make them blurrier.

The title isn't something I'd enter in a beauty contest, but it does show how creative you can be with layout. Make sure there's a creative reason for your title if you want to make something a little strange like the picture above. This will help it stick out against the background. Make sure the drop shadows or lines around the letters are thicker. No matter what, it doesn't help to have a title that people can't read. That's all there is to the wide world of Keynote titles. The app can do more than that, though. The steps tab is in the Animate tab, between the **Build-In and Build-Out** steps. You can now move any item on the screen along any motion path you want. This gives you a lot of options for making animations that look professional.

Creating path animations with Keynote

With keyframes, you can already move pictures and videos in iMovie, so why would you want to do it in Keynote?

Keynote animation is better than iMovie animation in three main ways, so if any of those are important to your project, you should use Keynote instead:

- You can export animations with see-through backgrounds;
- You can move more than one object at the same time;
- You can rotate objects to within one degree and rotate them around a path;

When it comes to titles, we've already seen how exporting with openness can help. Let's look at the other benefits of creating a small scene of a road in the country. Everything in the next picture was made in Keynote. You can see how the Keynote Pen tool, stock forms, and changes to the colors and gradients were used to make it. But for now, it's just a picture. You have to get some movement in the shot if you agree to take it on.

Our goal is to make it look like the car on the far left of the picture was driven across the road naturally. This can't be done in iMovie with a curvy road. By setting tens of thousands of keyframes, you can best make a form that appears bent. The car would follow the road, but it would not turn to follow the road. Instead, it would look like it was rolling the whole way.

To make the path in Keynote, follow these steps:

1. Click on the car. It has a bunch of shapes that are all grouped so that you can move them all at once.
2. Click Action in the **Animate** tab, then click Add an Effect.
3. For path movements, we need to click on the Move action. A faded copy of the car will be next to the real car, connected by a line.

The animation path is shown by the red line. The end of the animation path is shown by the faded car. If you click on the red diamond, you can add an animation. The path designer will open again after you click the diamond to turn off the Move motion.

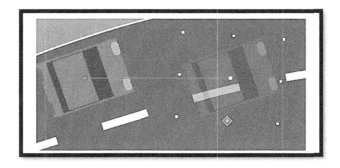

4. Click and drag the washed-out car to the end of the road. Like the real car, it should be facing the road in a way that makes sense.

The car's animation path is straight right now, but it's easy to add curves to make it follow the road:

5. There is a white circle (a keyframe) in the middle of the animation path when we move our mouse over it. Move the circle around until it lands where the road curves up the steepest (shown in circles in the picture).

6. You've moved the first white circle. When you move your mouse over the animation path, a new white circle will appear around the group of three trees.
7. Click and drag the new white circle to the bottom of the road, where it curves the sharpest. A square shows the area you should aim for.
8. From now on, the car will drive smoothly along the road from the beginning of the animation to the end. Go back to the **Animate sidebar** and check the **Align to Path** box. This will make the car turn in the right direction to follow the road like a real car would.

Even though it's a simple option, Align to Path is very useful. The path of the animation is now in order. But we still need to check that the speed is right and that the car looks like its going somewhere and coming from somewhere. **To do that, follow these steps:**

9. Click on the Animate sidebar again and change the Duration to a number longer than 5 seconds. This will make the car move more slowly. Press "Enter" to save the change in length.

Now, the car will drive along our road at a good speed. But right now, it's stopping and starting on the road. Do the following to make it look like the road the car has been on is just a small part of a bigger road:

10. Click on the square in the middle of the car that marks the beginning of the animation path and drag it off the slide. Use the **Shift Key + Command Key +, (comma)** to zoom out of the slide. This will help.
11. Do the same thing with the faded car at the end of the animation path.
12. Choose "**None**" from the drop-down menu next to "**Acceleration**." If you don't, it won't look like the car was moving before it entered the frame.

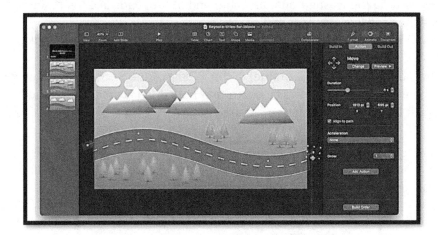

Click the **Build Order** button at the bottom of the Animate menu if you can't see the red diamond outside the frame slide after clicking off the animation path. The path will show up again after you click on the Build for the car (Group). Now it's time to look back and judge: as you watch the animation, look for times when the car leaves the road or goes too straight. Do these things to make the curve smoother:

13. Move your mouse over the motion line and click and drag a white circle to add another one. You might want to do the same thing further down the road to make the bend even again.

They always show up right in the middle of the two keyframes next to each other, which helps you find the white circle keyframes. These can be moved anywhere as long as they don't go over the next keyframe. But what about the other good thing about drawing in Keynote? It's easier to add more movements now that we know how to use them properly. To get those clouds moving, let's send another car the other way:

14. Press Command Key + C to copy the car, and then press Command Key + V to paste it on the other side of the road.
15. Click on Format on the left. To turn the car around and face the other way, click and drag the circle on the Rotate tool.

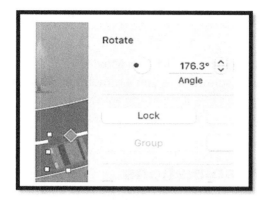

16. To remove the second car's motion path, go to the **Build Order menu** and press the backspace key. It's currently going the wrong way.
17. To make the second car's motion smooth, go back to steps 4–13 and click on **Animate | Action | Add an Effect | Move**. You can do it!
18. Change the second car to move with Build 1 in the Build Order menu. Then, add a delay to make the cars cross the road at different times.

Finally, let's clean up the clouds. Because there are so many, we'll make them all move at once:
19. Press the Shift key and click on each cloud to pick it. Then, go to Animate, Action, Add an Effect, and Move.
20. Change the Duration to at least 10 seconds and choose "None" for Acceleration.
21. Open the Build Order menu while the clouds are still chosen. Under the Start drop-down menu, choose With Previous Build.

Preview and evaluate: both cars should go on trips that look normal while clouds move slowly and imperceptibly above them. How pretty. Perhaps even lovelier is the fact that you made it all in Keynote. Check the steps again, especially steps 4–13, for making the motion path for the second car again if something is wrong. You'll need to change the keyframes so they fit in the other lane, but the idea is the same: put one keyframe at the top of the bend and one at the bottom of the bend.

Since there are no alpha channels in this scene, exporting this animation is much easier than it used to be:

22. To make a movie, go to **File > Export To > Movie**.
23. Click "**Next**" and save it somewhere you'll remember. There you have it!

We looked at animating more than one item at the same time near the end of this process. We'll look at the next motion feature that lets you do this, but this time with whole slides instead of pieces.

Using Magic Move animations

Magic Move is not the same as Magic Movie. It is a tool in Keynote that makes a smooth motion between slides by using the slides as keyframes. There is no state change for slide one when you add a Magic Move transition to it. It will look like slide two. This is a tool that is mostly used to easily spice up slide transitions, but it can also be used to animate video objects. Magic Move can do more than just handle all the movements on a screen at once. It can also help you get around some restrictions. For instance, when we use the Scale action on a very small form, the circle only gets a little bigger when the size is increased by 1,000%. So, if you wanted to make your transition, the circle would not be able to get big enough to cover the screen and hide the cut to the next clip. However, Magic Move would allow us to transition between slides if you had a small circle on one slide and the same circle enlarged to fill the whole slide on the next. This way of moving shapes is the basis for making custom transitions, so that's what we're going to do as our last job here.

But first, let us look at how to use Magic Move:

1. Click "**Add Slide**" in the Keynote menu, or press "**Shift Key + Command Key + N**" to quickly add a slide.

You might want to make a new basic presentation (**Command Key + N**) so you can start on slide one and stick to the slide numbers given.

2. Get rid of any text boxes on the slide.
3. Go to the menu and click **Shape**. Then, under **Basic**, click the **circle**.
4. You can change the color in the Format bar if you want to.
5. Hold down the Shift and Option keys and click on one of the squares around the circle. Then, drag the circle inwards.

Using the Shift Key and the Option Key together keeps the shape's lines of unity, so it doesn't get crooked or off. Make sure you let go of the click before you let go of the special keys when you're adjusting.

6. Use the Shift Key, the Command Key, and the "." key to zoom in on the slide as far as you can. This way, you can still see the circle when it gets really small. The shape's size is shown by a tooltip that hovers over it. Shrink the circle until it's about 5pt.

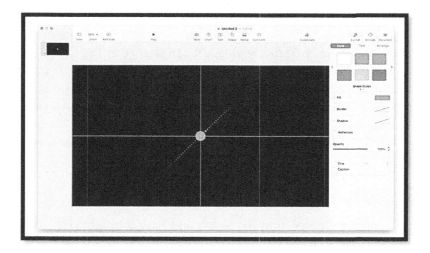

7. Click on the slide in the Slide Navigator on the left, and then press Command Key + D to make a copy of it.
8. Click the circle on the copied slide and drag it outward while holding down the Option and Shift keys. Do this until the circle fills the whole frame. To do this, you'll need to stop in the middle of the slide and zoom out (Shift Key + Command Key +.).

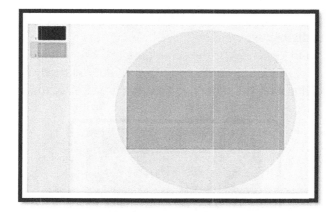

9. Go to the first slide again and click on the Animate part of the list.
10. Go to **Add an Effect** and click on **Magic Move**.

The small circle on the first slide should slowly get bigger until it covers the whole slide when you watch the Magic Move. That's the end of your first Magic Move. What does this have to do with making your transitions, though?

Custom transitions using overlays

An easy way to explain a transition is to say that it goes from clips one to clip two. Most transitions change the frame itself to make the change, like making the next clip less opaque until it takes over (dissolves) or removing or sliding the old clip off the screen. When we make this transition, though, we're making an object that will fill the frame. Because the thing in the middle of the screen is drawing attention away from the video, it can change in the background without the viewer's noticing. It might seem strange to go to such lengths to hide the cut, but it's useful if you want to transition to footage that people won't expect. These overlay transitions are often used in live sports to show a live repeat, which is both going back in time and showing the public something they've already seen. By making a noise like this, the transition helps people understand that their TVs haven't suddenly become stuck on repeat. That way, they can watch the live broadcast.

Creating simple transitions with Magic Move

Now that we know what animated transitions are and how they work, let's use the circle we animated with Magic Move to make one. We'll use the circle to block out the screen, and then use another Magic Move to put the circle back where it was. **We will then export the transition so that it can be used in iMovie.**

- If you haven't already, change your slides' background from Color Fill to No Fill in the Background drop-down box on the Format tab.
- Make a copy of the first slide and drag it to the bottom of Slide Navigator.
- The second slide is the one with the circle on the side. To change it, go to Animate, Add an Effect, and Magic Move.

Since Magic Moves aren't in the Build Order menu, we need to use Slide Navigator and the Animate tab to connect the builds.

- Press the Command Key and A at the same time to pick all the pictures.
- Setting the Start Transition drop-down button to automatically in the Animate tab. This transition works fine with the other settings that are already there.

We were able to link the motion to several slides by setting up various Magic Moves. There is no need to add two different animation lines for the same object on the same slide. This makes the animation easier to edit and understand at a glance. But since Magic Moves doesn't have any build order settings, you can't move different things at different times. This means you will need to use the normal animation actions if you want two animations to interact with each other by crossing over and out of time for visual interest.

Exporting and importing multi-stage Magic Move animations

The export process changes to include a range of slides since we're using more than one. This is what you need to do to export your Magic Move transition:

1. Click on File, then Export To, and then Movie.
2. Pick the right number of slides. Either All or Slides 1 through 3 will work in a new Keynote file.
3. Choose "Custom" from the choice that drops down.
4. Pick HEVC as the compression type and check the box next to Export with clear backgrounds.
5. Click "Next," give the place a good name, and save it.

It's time to import your three-slide range into iMovie after exporting it as a video with transparency. Do these things in iMovie:

1. Use the Command Key + I import menu to bring in your saved transition.
If you made an Event for your animations, select it from the drop-down menu in the center of the Import menu.
2. Add two clips to the timeline that are very different from each other, like a red and green background, to test the transition.
3. Move the middle of the transition clip over the edit place where the two clips meet. This will add the clip as an overlay.
4. Move your mouse over the transition overlay and press C. Then press / (forward slash). This picks the clip and only plays the transition.
5. The circle should fill the frame at that point, so you shouldn't see the clip in the main video layer change colors. If the transition worked, you'll see the circle grow over it. The overlay clip might need to be moved to make sure it does this.
You won't get a cool transition because it's only one circle. However, it does a good job of getting people's attention. From what we've seen so far, this is just the beginning of what we can learn

more about. You can use your creativity to make titles and images that show who you are as a maker or what your video is about now that you know how to use the tools. The last type of animation we'll look at is a lot easier and almost does itself.

Dead easy animation with Dynamic Backgrounds

Dynamic Backgrounds were added in Keynote version 12.1. They let you choose a set of colors that will move the background of your slide. If you need to fill in some blank space in a video but don't have any B-roll, a moving background will look a little more interesting than a still picture that is kept for a long time. There's no better way to make a video than to include interesting and relevant footage, but having an active background on hand is always a good idea.

To create and export one, follow these instructions:

1. Press the Command Key and N to make a new Keynote show.
2. Pick Dynamic Rainbow (or Dynamic Dark for a darker background; you can change all the colors in the motion with either one).
3. In the Format panel, there is a color bar that shows how the screen changes from one color to another. If you click on the marks, you can change the colors.
4. If you move your mouse over the color bar and click on an empty spot, you can add more colors.

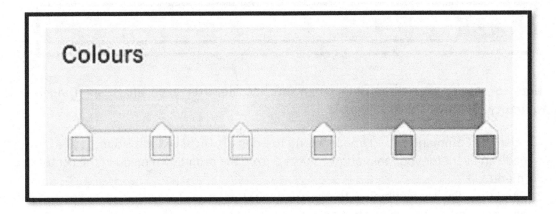

5. **You can also change the following in the Format panel:**
   - **Scale**: The number that tells you how close the colors are on the slide and how far apart they are.
   - **Speed**: The speed at which the colors move on the screen
6. Export the changing background as a normal 1080p video when you're satisfied. As long as you set the time for "**Go to next slide after**" in the export menu, that's how long the video will be.
7. You could store these images in iMovie by making an event for them (Option Key + N).

Export Your Presentation

PDF   PowerPoint   Movie   Animated GIF   Images   HTML   Keynote '09

Playback: Self-Playing

Slides: ○ All
From: 1   to   1

Go to next slide after: [17]   seconds

Go to next build after: 2.0   seconds

Timings apply only to click events.

Resolution: 1080p

Works best for playing movies on iPad with Retina display and Apple TV.

?   Cancel   Next...

And those are changeable backgrounds that you can use right away if you need to edit a video quickly. There's no reason why you should have to go through that, though. With everything you've learned, you can make the video you want.

CHAPTER 14

CUSTOM EXPORT FORMATS, FT. HANDBRAKE

No more coming up with ideas. It's time to make changes to our video master copy so that it can be exported to different places. That was a bit of a philosophical statement. We've talked about how to make your video clear, to the point, and full of extra information, meaning, and your style. It sounds good now, and we added some extra effects to keep people interested. Our video is great, but it won't work for everyone.

Working with aspect ratio

A video's aspect ratio shows how long it is compared to how tall it is. For a 16:9 screen, the screen goes 9 pixels up for every 16 pixels (or any other number) that we move along it. A 4:3 frame will be higher than a 16:9 frame, so if you overlayed 4:3 footage over 16:9 footage, pillar boxes, which are the sides of the 16:9 video below, would show through. Different aspect ratios will give a video frame a different general shape. One would have to be cropped to make it shorter, and the other would have to be cropped to make it taller. This is so that both videos fit in the same-sized frame.

Aspect ratio examples

This is what aspect ratio looks like in real life, to give you an idea: 16:9 is the standard for HD TV today. Old TV shows were shot in 4:3, which is higher than 16:9. Column boxes show up on the sides of a 16:9 screen. Widescreen movies can be as wide as 2.39:1, which makes the picture shorter and wider than on most TVs. This makes letterboxes above and below the picture on a 16:9 screen. > MacBook screens are 16:10, which is a little higher than 16:9, so when you watch movies in full screen, they leave small letterboxes. Not only will that, but the sharpness of a screen tell you what its aspect ratio is. It will be if you have a full HD (1920x1080) frame.

- 1,920 pixels long and 1,080 pixels tall
- If we simplify 1,920 and 1,080, we get:
  - **192:108** (1,920 and 1,080 both divided by 10)
  - **16:9** (192 and 108 both divided by 12)

For example, if you had a video of your phone screen that was 720 pixels long and 1,280 pixels high, you would get 72:128. Then, you would get 9:16 by dividing both 72 and 128 by 8. Please excuse the large number load; it's helpful to see how resolution and aspect ratio are connected. The aspect ratio of the frame can be found in any format that is sped up as much as possible. **This is how you can see the aspect ratio of a video on macOS, along with a lot of other information:**

1. Right-click on a video files and choose "Open With" from the menu that comes up.
2. Press the **Command Key and the letter I** to open the Video Inspector.
3. Click on the drop-down button next to Video Details

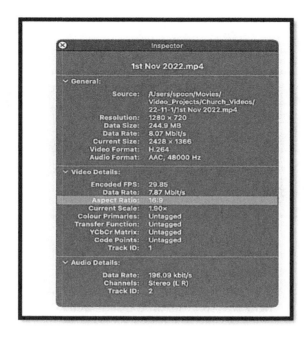

4. Don't pay attention to the information about the **Current Scale**. Anything that starts with "**Current**" refers to the size of the video window you have opened on your Mac, not the video itself.

We've seen that iMovie will only export your video in 16:9, no matter what shape the clip is. You have to change the aspect ratio outside of the app if you need to. A transcoder lets you change the aspect ratio of your video, which is what we'll look at next. But you can also use Keynote, which lets you export slides in any aspect ratio you want, which we know can be used as the frame of our video.

Changing aspect ratio with Keynote

First, it's important to note that Keynote is not an NLE, no matter how powerful it is. Before we change the aspect ratio of our video, we need to make sure we're happy with it and then export a master copy from iMovie. This is how we should always use software that is made for that purpose. **To sum up, the following should be on the master copy:**

- The best resolution that can be found (what you set the project's resolution to)
- The best quality possible (ProRes if you have room, or Custom quality to the right if you don't):

In iMovie, "Quality" refers to the bit rate of the video. I'll say more about that later. **After exporting the video, we can bring it back into Keynote and change the way it looks. That's easy to do:**

1. Press the Command Key and N to start a new simple Keynote project.
2. Click the Document button on the far right part of the menu to open the Document box.

3. From the drop-down box next to Slide Size, choose Custom Slide Size...
4. Change the numbers for Width and Height to get the aspect ratio you want:

5. To return to the slide, click OK or press Enter. It will look different now.
6. From the Finder, drag and drop a video file onto the Keynote slide. The video will appear as a clip that you can resize and that has a play button in the middle.
7. Make the video the right size so it fits on the slide and lines up with the yellow lines of equal length:
   - If your video is bigger than the aspect ratio you chose (this is called "pillarboxing"), you need to make sure that the height of the slide is exactly the right size.
   - Make sure you fill in the exact length of the slide if your video is higher than the aspect ratio you set (this is called "letterboxing" the video).

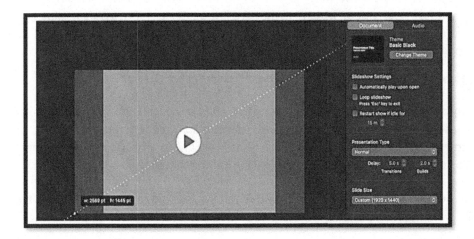

8. Click on **File**, then **Export To**, and then **Movie**.
9. You can also change the video's frame rate from the Keynote export menu if you need to.

The aspect ratio you export is based on the slide size that you set earlier. However, we still need to set the resolution to make sure that Keynote doesn't lower the quality of our video.

1. You'll need to change the size to Custom if your wide resolution is more than 1,080 pixels, which it probably is. Edit the numbers so they match the size of the slide you chose.

2. Click the **next** button... Save the file somewhere you'll remember with a name you'll remember.

Hey presto, the video is now the right size! One easy way to change the aspect ratio of your video is to use Keynote. When you export, any parts of your video that are outside the slide are cut off, kind of like how you use a shredder to cut paper to size. So, if you made a video that was only in portrait mode, you could drag it into Keynote, change the slide size to something like 1080x1920, and then export only the portrait footage. But that's not good because most of the frame is lost no matter what export size you choose. There is a way to keep all of the sharpness in portrait movies.

Exporting sideways from iMovie

When we look at aspect ratios, we can see that a portrait screen (9:16) is the opposite of an HD widescreen (16:9). It's like the height and length have been switched. This means that 16:9 footage that is in landscape mode only needs to be turned 90 degrees to become portrait mode. This is something you can do in iMovie. For this method to work, you have to turn all of your picture footage 90 degrees so that it lies on its side. After saving, you can use QuickTime Player to turn the video around so it is now facing the right way. This is better because when you export from iMovie, the whole frame is filled. Because of this, a 1920x1080 portrait video made this way will look better than one made by cutting out most of a 1920x1080 frame in Keynote. If you can, edit your clips normally and then flip them right before you export. This will help you edit better since you won't have to tilt your head to look at the computer screen. **But before you begin, there are some things you should remember:**
- When you edit, all of the clips you use must be portrait. If you only rotate a portrait part of the video, QuickTime Player will flip most of the video over when you're done.
- When you rotate the clips, they must all be rotated in the same way.
- When you rotate clips, Crop to fill boxes and Ken Burns effects will start over.

Still want to use this method? You'll need to rotate the clips before you start editing them if you need to use crop boxes and Ken Burns' animations. It won't work quite the same way after that, though. **To export and fix a portrait video, follow these steps:**
1. Change as many of your picture clips as you can to the way they were meant to be edited.

2. Make a list of all the clips you want to use crop effects on right away (M).
3. Select a clip and click on the Crop menu in the toolbar. Then, click on the left-hand rotate button:
    - You can turn the clip any way you want, as long as you also turn the other clips the same way. We'll stick with a counterclockwise (to the left) turn in iMovie for this example:

4. Choose a crop style, such as Crop to fill or Ken Burns, based on the type of resizing you want.

Here's where things could go wrong, though. There is a 16:9 aspect ratio set in the crop boxes, so they won't move when you use them on a flipped video. In real life, this means you can't have a crop box that goes all the way to the top of the frame unless you want to show the whole video. This is shown in the picture below; remember to edit this while looking sideways at the frame:

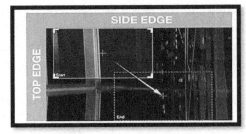

It's a little hard to be creative with this, but I hope it won't stop you from using zooming and resizing to do what you want to. If it does, you'll need to edit and export your portrait video normally, and then use Keynote to cut the sides off. **However, keep in mind that doing so will affect the quality. Let's go back to the main steps:**
1. Do steps 3 through 4 again for all of the clips that were marked.
2. Press the **Command Key** and click on all the clips that aren't marked.
3. Select the **Crop menu** and choose the **Rotate the clip counterclockwise** option.
It's time to export your clips now that they've all been turned properly and your edits have been saved.
1. In the menu bar, go to **File | Share | File**:
In this case, you can get to the same place as if you clicked the Share button and then Export File.

2. Set all the settings to the maximum, just like you would for any other master export.

3. Click "Next" and save the file temporarily, like on your desktop.
4. Double-click the file to open it in QuickTime Player when the copying is done.
5. To turn the video back to horizontal mode, press the Shift Key, the Command Key, and the R keys at the same time.

In iMovie, you can rotate all of your movies clockwise. To spin a video to the left in QuickTime Player, press Shift + Command + L.

6. Follow the on-screen instructions to save the video after editing it.

That's all there is to making a picture export in iMovie. You can change the aspect ratio of your saved video using this fix or the Keynote way we already talked about. But you'll need to use a transcoder like Handbrake if you want to change video details like file types or make a version of your video export that fits into a certain file size.

How to install and run Handbrake

To change the aspect ratio of our video in Keynote, we had to encode a new video. This meant that Keynote created and uploaded a new video file. However there is a different way to change the aspect ratio and that is to transcode the source video, which changes information about it. This part will teach you how to set up Handbrake and use it. Handbrake is something we'll get from somewhere other than the App Store. Handbrake is a free, open-source app that lets you change how movies are released. We'll be using it to change our videos into different forms so they can be exported. The website for **Handbrake is https://handbrake.fr/**, and you can find it on **GitHub at https://github.com/HandBrake/HandBrake**. After getting Handbrake, the first thing we need to do is make sure it's in the Applications folder.

To be sure, do the following:

1. For Handbrake, the file you'll get is a DMG. The file will grow into a Volume when you double-click it. A Volume is not the same thing as a sound; a Volume is just a storage device you can remove from your computer:

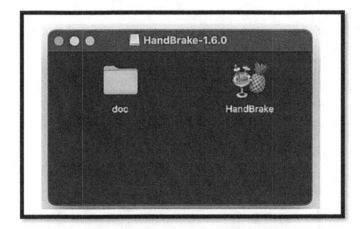

2. The app is HandBrake, which you can see on the right. The key for this is Command + Shift + A. It needs to be moved to the Applications folder. It will copy to Applications if you drag the app there.
3. After the copying is done, it's time to get rid of the downloaded files. Right-click on the Volume and choose "**Eject**" from the menu that comes up. The DMG file can also be deleted.
4. To open **HandBrake**, go to the **Applications** area and double-click on it. You can also use Spotlight (**Command Key + Spacebar**) to look for the app and press **Enter** when it comes up. The app's screen will look like the picture below when it opens:

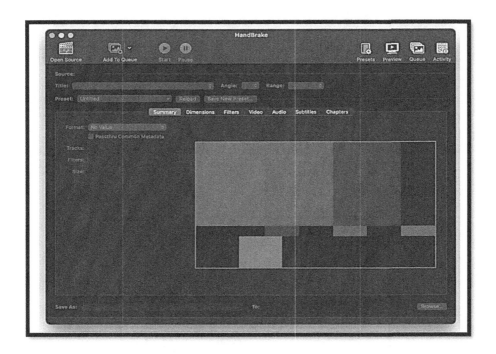

Adding a source to Handbrake

Handbrake requires a source video that will make changes to transcode. There you have it, the master export from iMovie. You can add a source video to Handbrake in a few different ways:

- Pick a video file from the Finder window that appears when you open the app.
- In the top left corner of the Handbrake window, click the **Open Source** button. That will bring up the Finder menu where you can pick out a file.

The Handbrake interface has a lot to look at, and it can be hard to know where to begin. That's why we'll start with just the most important parts. First, let's look at how to use the Dimensions tab to change the aspect ratio of movies.

Changing video cropping in Handbrake

You can crop pixels from each side of the video you add with Handbrake. This lets you change the aspect ratio of your video to any size you want. **When you're ready to transcode a file in Handbrake:**

1. Look for a row of tabs at the top of the window that lets you move around. These change what the screen shows and let you change different parts of the video. Select "**Dimensions**."

2. The next step is to look for some options on the left that say **"Orientation and Cropping."** Change the **Cropping setting** from **Automatic to Custom** using the drop-down menu that appears.

3. After being grayed out, four boxes with different amounts should become clear. In terms of pixels, these show how much the video is being cropped at the top, right, bottom, and left (read them clockwise):

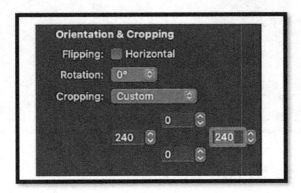

4. The numbers may already be in the boxes because Handbrake automatically crops. This automatic tool is very smart; it looks for empty spots in the video that can be cut out, like letterboxes and pillar boxes.

This will work great sometimes. Change all of these numbers to 0 for now, though, to be sure you're getting the right aspect ratio.

5. To get the right cutting for the ratio, we need to figure out how many pixels we need to cut off the top or sides. From the difference between the two image sizes, we can tell. The size of a full HD 16:9 video would change from **1920x1080 to 1440x1080** if we changed it to 4:3. This means we're cutting:
   - 240 pixels off of each side (for a total of 480)
   - 0 pixels off the top and bottom

6. Press **"Enter"** to save the changes to the crop. These are the new video's file size and aspect ratio that will be shown under the **"Final Dimensions"** heading near the bottom of the Handbrake window:

The Aspect Ratio reading will change every time you crop, so this part of the Handbrake window is useful to check. If it gives you a strange number that doesn't match the aspect ratio you know, that's a good sign that you should check the cropping again.

Exporting from Handbrake

Now that the final sizes are right, pick a place to send the video and transcode it. That's easy to do:

1. The Save As option is at the bottom of the Handbrake window. Click on the box that says "File Name," and then pick a name that is different from the original, like "file_transcoded.mp4":

2. There will be a file path next to the filename that tells you where to save the converted file. Press the **Browse** button and pick a different save spot in Finder to change this.
3. Click the green "**Start**" button at the top of the Handbrake window to begin the transcoding. The app will give you a rough idea of how long the transcode will take.

If your file doesn't end up where you expect. Even after setting an export spot, Handbrake doesn't always place the transcoded files where they belong. You can use the Queue window to find the files if they aren't where you thought they would be. **This window helps keep track of your encodes anyway:**

1. To start the queue, click **Queue** at the top of the Hole box.
2. Right-click on the file you want to find in the list on the left. It will show the new name you gave the encoded file.
3. You can find out a lot about the transcoding job in the panel on the right side of the window. Under "**Summary**," it says where the transcoded file will go.

If you only need to change the aspect ratio of one video, Keynote is still probably your best bet. It's easier to use, and it comes with macOS. Cropping and adjusting the video is also easier to understand because you're using a clip of the video and a slide as a guide. But that doesn't mean you should never use a transcoder. One of the main times you might need a transcoder is to make changes to several video files at once.

Transcoding multiple files with Handbrake

Handbrake works best when you need to convert a lot of files at once, even if each video has different settings. **To convert more than one file at once, we need to make a queue. That's easy to do:**

1. Choose the first file you want to convert in the Finder box after opening Handbrake.

2. In Handbrake, you can change the settings that matter in the different tabs. For example, you can change the aspect ratio in Dimensions.
3. Change the file's name and where it will be saved by using the Save As option.
4. On the menu for the handbrake, click "Add to Queue."

5. Choose the second file you want to transcode and click "Open Source." Does Steps 2 through 5 again for as many files as you want to transcode?
6. Click **Start Queue** when you're done adding all the sources you want. Every video in the queue will be transcoded by Handbrake.

When processing several files at once, the Queue window makes it easy to keep an eye on how each one is going and see if there are any problems. The convert process will stop if Handbrake can't handle a file. It will then move on to the next thing on the list. There are other ways to add more than one video to a transcoding file besides the one we looked at. The settings can also be saved as a preset, which can then be used on folders full of files.

Using presets in Handbrake

It might not be possible to change the transcoder's settings for every single file that needs to be changed if you have a lot of them. The good news is that Handbrake has a Preset drop-down menu that lets you change the video and sound quality settings based on the platform and format you want to compress a video for.

The quick 1080p30 setting is what it's called by default (1920x1080 resolutions, 30 frames per second). Here are a few platform-specific forms you might want to check out:

*   **Preset | Web | Discord Small 2 Minutes 360p30**
*   **Preset | Web | Gmail Large 3 Minutes 720p30**

You can use these presets to make your video file smaller than the free file upload limits for Gmail (25 MB) and Discord (8 MB). Check out the different Handbrake choices to see what settings change when you choose these. Setting your standards is a valuable learning exercise.

Creating presets in Handbrake

You can enter settings into Handbrake and save them as a preset. You can then use this preset on any video you want. Say I have a folder full of old movies. All of them were exported in 16:9, but the original recording was made on an iPad, which has a 4:3 screen.

So, I want a setup that will get rid of the pillar boxes on the sides of all of them:

1. Open Handbrake and pick a file from the Finder window that fits.
2. Make sure that the main preset is set to Fast 1080p30, which is the default. It's a good base to build on; some of the custom conditions that Handbrake adds to other settings can make your encodes not work.
3. To see the dimensions, click the tab.
4. To crop, switch to Custom and cut 240 pixels off the left and right sides.
5. There will now be a 4:3 aspect ratio after you press Enter to save the changes.
6. Click Save New Preset in the Preset menu.

When you make a template, a window will pop up that lets you add more information:

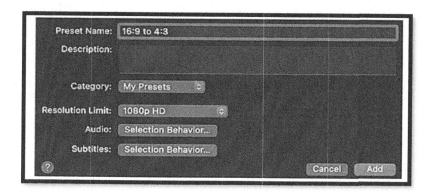

7. It is important to keep the 1080p HD quality limit because the cropping we chose only works for 1920x1080 movies. Don't worry about the other settings for now.
8. To make the setting, click "**Add**."
9. Now, move your mouse over the "**My Presets**" option at the bottom of the "**Preset**" drop-down menu. The setting you saved will always be there for you to use whenever you want.

We can use the preset on many movies that all need to be transcoded in the same way now that we've made it.

Batch-transcoding a folder of videos

We're going to add to our previous use of our Queue by adding a bunch of movies that will be transcoded using our preset:

1. In Finder, make sure that all of the files you want to convert are in the same folder.

2. Select the folder with the movies in Finder and drag and drop it over the Handbrake window. The source movies you added will be scanned in by Handbrake.
3. From the "**Preset**" drop-down box, choose the preset you want to use.
4. Use the Browse... menu to pick a place to save all the new files. It would be helpful to make a new folder for the transcoded files since you are changing many files at once.

We can put together the queue now that the settings and location are correct:
1. Put all of the movies in a queue. To add titles to the queue, go to **File | Add Titles to Queue** or press **Shift + Command** + B on the computer.
2. A list with checkboxes for each file in the folder will show up. At this time, you can click on the video's filename to remove it from the queue:

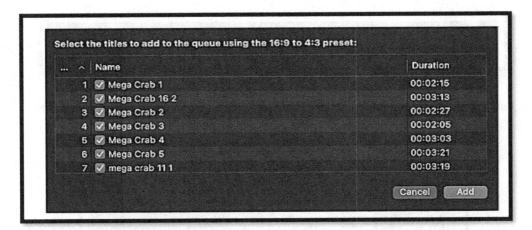

3. Use the current converting settings to add all the movies in the folder to the list. You can click "Add" or press "Enter."
4. **On the menu for the handbrake, click Start Queue:**
   ∞ You might want to wait before you do this. Check out the next part for some compression tips that you can try out on a new setting.

We can now convert movies all at once, which is helpful when you need to work with a lot of files at once. With a transcoder, we can change more than just the aspect ratio, though. People usually use a transcoder when they want to change more than one thing about a video. Transcoders are best known for shrinking file sizes, which will be useful if you want to share master copies of your video in multiple locations. You can change the aspect ratio and file size of your video using different tabs in Handbrake.

Using Handbrake to compress files

It is possible to make something smaller by getting rid of information that makes it better. This is called compression. Why would we ever want to make our video less good? Well, if you've saved movies from iMovie in ProRes, you know that master video copies are very large. There are file size limits that you need to follow on many websites and other places, like clients. If file size isn't a problem, we can use the best copy of our video that we have because we have a master copy. I said I'd talk about why ProRes files are so much bigger, so here it is.

What is ProRes?

Although we won't go into the details of video compression, it's helpful to understand why **Best Quality (ProRes)** video is so much bigger than exporting with the Custom slider set to the highest quality in iMovie. For people who know a lot about videos, this is a very simple description, but the important lesson is still there. Almost all videos are reduced because they have to be. Video files would be too big to keep, stream, or even play if they weren't compressed. With inter-frame compression, frames are skipped and guesses are made about what will happen in those frames instead of the information being stored. Choosing the start, middle, and end points of a path and animating in between them is the same as drawing a path with keyframes. The only difference is that the path being animated is the compression algorithm's best guess. As it were, it guesses because those things take up a lot less room than real video data. Why? The encoder needs all the pixel information in a frame to record and store all the information about that frame. Just think about how many pixels are in 1920x1080. That should help you understand. Because compression algorithms are so good at guessing between keyframes, most of the time we don't even notice that the quality of the movies we watch has been lost. Everything goes along with the flow of the video, as it should. But ProRes is made so that it doesn't have to guess. It does reduce movies in other ways, but it doesn't mess around with guesses. **This has two effects:**

- The video quality is almost lossless
- It's easier and faster to edit with

Wait. If ProRes files are much larger and hold much more information, how on Earth can they be less taxing on your computer? That's because your NLE doesn't have to guess what keyframes are for. It already knows about all the frames, so it can import, process, and export video more quickly. Not sure about this? If you want to export a video from iMovie, choose **High Quality** and then **Best (ProRes).** Some Macs, like those with an M-series chip, have parts of the chip that are designed to make ProRes work faster. This means that the export will go faster. And that's what ProRes is. Because it's almost perfect, it's the best way to export your video's master copy. ProRes is useful for more than just NLEs, though. Also, transcoders like Handbrake can work with a ProRes master file better since they can see all the frame information. This lets them skip frames and quickly come up with better ideas.

Compressing video with Handbrake

There are more ways to use a transcoder to reduce file size than either of us could ever count, so let's focus on some guaranteed ways to reduce the size of your video:

- Use the H.265 codec
- Use Handbrake's suggested quality range
- Leave the audio alone

Let's go through each of these rules in turn.

Use the H.265 codec

The word "**codec**" comes from the words "**encode" and "decode**." Codecs tell computers how to encode and receive video and audio files. H.264 is without a doubt the best video codec standard. It's all over the place and has been since 2003. When H.265 was added to the standard in 2013, it made it better. You may know this better as HEVC on Apple products. This is the codec we used to export Keynote slides, and you can also use it to save movies with QuickTime Player. A group of instructions called H.265 tells computers to do the same thing that H.264 does, but faster. That means the files will be smaller but still look good. **The following steps can be taken to change the format that Handbrake uses:**

1. Startup Handbrake and go to the Video tab.
2. Pick H.265 (x265) from the Video Encoder drop-down box.

Quality range in Handbrake

This button is to the right of the Video Encoder window in Handbrake. A number called RF is used for H.265. The video quality is better when the RF is smaller, but the file size is bigger. The reason for this is that it's using more of the source video's data and guessing less. Things are different when the RF is higher. **This is what Handbrake suggests you do, and it changes depending on the video's resolution:**

- RF 18-22 for 480p (Standard Definition)
- RF 19-23 for 720p (HD)
- RF 20-24 for 1080p (Full HD)
- RF 22-28 for 2160p (4K)

From this scale, you can see that the fewer data you need to keep for a video to still have good picture quality, the better the resolution. For example, if you stick to RF 20, you can copy a full HD video and get a copy that is very close to the original in terms of quality while saving file size. Because it is more efficient, the H.265 codec will save even more space on files.

Leave audio alone

This one is pretty easy to understand. As a way to save space, don't lower the quality of the audio. This is because of two things:

- Audio takes up very little space in a file
- As humans, we notice (and dislike) a drop in sound quality more strongly than a drop in video quality

Don't change the audio settings. The sound is only a small part of the video file, and we all love good sound. Any reduction in file size will make the experience worse for the viewers. Now that we've talked about these different factors, let's use them by making one of your master files smaller.

Creating a ProRes export from a mobile project

These steps will show you how to export a project from iMovie for iOS or iPadOS, import it into iMovie for macOS, and then export it again as a master copy. First, on your phone or tablet:

1. Start up the iMovie app.
2. Tap on your project to see a bigger picture of it.
3. Click on the Share button in the middle.
4. At the top of the Share box, tap Options.
5. Select "**Project**" as the Type and press "Back" to leave the window.
6. On both your phone and your computer, make sure Bluetooth is on and AirDrop is set to receive:

The Control Center is in the upper right corner of the screen. This is where you can findAirDrop settings. You'll need to swipe down with one finger on a phone.

7. Go back to your phone and tap AirDrop at the top of the Share menu. Then, when your Mac shows up under Devices, tap it.

It's possible to export your whole video to your Mac in these first steps. The clips will still be in place, so you can edit them again. Now, use the.iMovieMobile files you saved to open the Berlin project on your Mac. **This is the file you sent to yourself:**

- On your Mac, open iMovie.
- Click on File and then Import iMovie iOS Projects.
- Find the file called .iMovieMobile. Finder will show grayed-out files that iMovie can't open because it can't handle them. If you sent the file through AirDrop, it will be in Downloads (pressing Option Key + Command Key + L).
- Pick out the file and click "Import." When you start a new project in iMovie, the timeline will be set up exactly the way you had it in the mobile app.
- Click File, Share, and then File again if you're happy with the video.
- Set the quality to Best (ProRes) and the size to 1080p for the project. Also, make sure that Compression is set to Better Quality:

We can now shrink the size of the ProRes export so that it's easier to work with. Let's put it in Handbrake and follow the three rules we already talked about.

Compressing a master video with Handbrake

How much you need to compress a file will depend on the website you're using or the person you're making a video for. But following the three rules for compression will get you a very watchable copy of the video that is also much smaller. **Now let's start to shrink our master export:**

1. Open Handbrake and in the Finder window, choose your master export.
2. Click on the **Video** tab and pick **H.265 (x265)** from the Video Encoder drop-down box.
3. The **Quality setting** set by default, **RF22**, is fine for a **1080p** video, so let's leave it that way.
4. The usual setting, fast **1080p30**, doesn't change the sound in a bad way, but make sure there is only one audio track mentioned in the **Sound** tab. If there are two, use the drop-down choice to make the second one "**None.**" The second bar shows stereo audio (two separate channels), which **iMovie** does not export:

5. In the **Save As** box, give the file a name that you can remember and choose a good place to save it.
6. To start the translation process, click **Start** in the menu.

You can change another setting in Handbrake if the time it says the process will take (shown on the app icon) is too long. You can choose a faster compression setting to speed up the process, but the file will be bigger because it will not be as efficient.

- On the Handbrake menu, click Stop. In the window that comes up, click Stop All.
- Go back to the Video tab and leave the Preset bar two places to the left in Encoder Options.

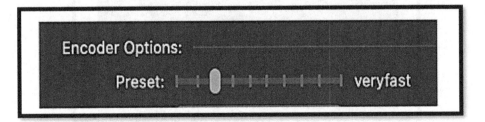

- Press the Start button on the Handbrake menu once more.
- When the encoding is done, open Finder and compare the new file's size to that of the master export to see if the file size has shrunk.

The size of my ProRes "Berlin" export shrunk from 1.12 GB to 17.1 MB, a drop of over 98%. If you compressed from a ProRes file, you should see the same drop. What if we want to compress the file even more, though? To do this, we can use a clearer measure of quality.

Compressing to a specific size with bitrate controls

There is a pattern to the size of your video file. A lot of it has to do with how long it is and how fast it is compressed. We can change the bitrate to get a better idea of the file size for our video.

The bitrate tells us how much data is in the video per second. Here's how to figure out the bitrate:

- **((Bitrate [kbps] = File size [MB] / (file length [minutes] * 0.0075))**

Let's look at a case study. I need to know the file size if I want my Berlin summary to fit inside 8 MB. The time is 1:15 minutes, which is 1.25 minutes. Since 0.0075 is a fixed number that's always in the calculation, let's finish the calculation for my Berlin video by figuring out what's in the brackets first:

- Bitrate [kbps] = 8 [MB] /(1.25 [minutes] *0.0075)
- Bitrate = 8/0.009375
- Bitrate = 853 kbps

At that rate, my video would take up 853 kbps of space. That can be set in Handbrake like this:
- Click on the Video tab.
- Go to the Quality area and click on the circle that says Average Bitrate (kbps). It doesn't matter what the RF number is now.
- Enter the bitrate you found in the box and press Enter. Do not uncheck the boxes:

- Check that the height and width are still 1080p and that the video encoder is still set to H.265 (x265).

- On the menu for the Handbrake, click "**Start**."

You might find that the file is a little bigger than you thought it would be when the encoding is done (editing is never an exact science!). Cut down on the average speed and try the encode again if you need to get the video under a certain size.

Disadvantages of using Average Bitrate

With the **Average Bitrate** option, you can get a file to almost the exact size you want, but it's not the best way to do it. The **Constant Quality** option is what Handbrake suggests, and there are some problems with encoding with **Average Bitrate**:

- Video quality is not a number; it's a matter of opinion. The watcher will benefit more from a steady quality than an average rate of information.
- Figuring out the file size doesn't give exact results because the video time and size aren't the only ones that matter. This means that getting a file to the right size can still take a lot of trial and error, even with this method.
- When you encode with an average bitrate instead of steady quality, it takes longer. This is because the transcoder has to do the process twice to make sure that parts of the video with more color changes and movement get more data.
- Using bitrate to shrink the file size can ruin the quality of the video if it is done too much. If you want to save room, you can sometimes use the Dimensions menu to lower the size.

With these problems in mind, it's most likely best to stick with Constant Quality whenever you can. But that's all there is to say about the compression process. Hopefully, this part has helped you understand how video compression works and how you can use Handbrake to quickly and effectively shrink files.

CHAPTER 15

TROUBLESHOOTING AND FAQS

Common iMovie Problems and Their Solutions

What the iMovie user guide doesn't say is what the program does wrong. With some changes, there may be a note that a bug has been fixed, but the gremlins that keep bothering users aren't mentioned. As a result, we iMovie producers keep having these issues.

Problem – iMovie won't accept your video format

There are times when iMovie won't accept the files you've taken or won't play them correctly right from the start of a project. Most likely, these issues are caused by limitations in the import process. However, iMovie can sometimes just not work well with the videos you want to use. First, let's look at iMovie's file types and limits. **There are a few different ways that iMovie can say that it doesn't like certain files:**
- When you drag and drop the video in, a "no entry" icon will show up and the video won't show up in the timeline.
- If you try to import a video with Command Key + I, the video file will be grayed out and you won't be able to choose it.

Many of the video files you use won't have this issue, but iMovie doesn't like some video cases (the letters at the end of the title). Other programs, like VLC Player, and most NLEs do not have any problems with them. **These are the iMovie trouble categories that come up most often:**
- **avi** (Audio Video Interleave – the original Windows video file container)
- **.mkv** (Matroska video)
- **.webm** (web media – this can be video or audio)

But containers aren't the only thing that matters. MKV and the VP8/VP9/AV1 codecs are examples of containers that work with certain codecs. However, different codecs can be used with different containers. For the file types that iMovie supports (M4V, MOV, and MP4), the video file may have been compressed with a codec that iMovie doesn't like. The video won't work then.

Solution – transcoding video that iMovie won't accept

It would be hard to keep track of all the types that work with iMovie because there are so many of them. Since iMovie won't let you import movies, the only real option is to convert them. **Handbrake is a good tool for this job because it can be used for many things:**
- Put the handbrake on.
- In the Finder box, pick out your video and click "Open." The folder for the transcoded file will be set to MP4 in the Summary tab under Format. We'll leave this as is because it works well with other programs.

- Handbrake will automatically set to the fast 1080p30 mode. If the quality of your video is higher than 1080p, go to the Dimensions tab and use the quality Limit drop-down choice to make the limit bigger to fit your video.
- If your video's frame rate isn't 30 FPS, go to the Video tab and choose its frame rate from the drop-down menu next to Famerate (FPS):
    - It looks like the "Same as Source" option would be the best choice, but it's not very stable and can often make the encoding process fail.
- To keep the video's quality, move the Quality bar to one of the following settings while you're still in the Video tab:
- RF19 for a 720p video, RF20 for a 1080p video, and RF22 for a 4K video.
- Pick an appropriate place and name for the exported file in the Save As area at the bottom of the Handbrake window.
- Click "**Start**" to start the process of transcoding.

This method can be useful if iMovie won't let you import a video, but it can also be used as a backup. Running your video files through Handbrake before editing them can be helpful if you aren't sure if the folder and codec are compatible with iMovie. For example, if you took the video on an iPhone or iPad, they would be. This normally gets rid of any issues that were inactive but would cause a lot of trouble later on in the edit.

Problem – clips don't play properly

There are times when movies that seem to be loaded correctly will not work right. To be safe, it's a good idea to run movies through a transcoder first, then import them. But if movies you've already imported won't play, there are some things you can try that might "remind" iMovie of the video it should be playing.

Solution – "reminding" iMovie of the clips in the project

Follow these steps:

- Use Finder to find the media that won't play right.
- Click on the file and hold it over the iMovie timeline while you drag it in. You don't have to drop it in. If iMovie has "forgotten" something about the file and won't play it right, you can get it to work again by showing it the original file.
- In the same way, you can try loading the same media again by pressing Command Key + I and going to the import menu.

It might help to copy the schedule into a new project if that doesn't work:

- Press Command Key + A and Command Key + C to copy all the clips in the timeline.
- Press 2 to return to the Projects page, and then press Command Key + N to make a new project.
- Use Command Key + V to paste all the clips into the timeline of the new project.

Here are some common computer repair tips that might help if that doesn't work anymore:
- Quit iMovie and start it again
- Restart your computer

This whole situation shows how important it is to keep your original video files in Finder while you edit them. It also shows how useful it is to encode your media before loading it. But clips also have another problem that a lot of people have. The clip folder and format may be fine, and the import begins. But for some reason, it stops in the middle, and iMovie says it is still trying to download movies from iCloud.

Problem – iCloud videos are still "downloading"

iMovie users, mostly those who use iMovie for iOS or iPadOS, are having a lot of trouble with this. When you choose media from the Media Browser to add to a project, the clips don't go there. The app says that the media (mostly movies) is still being downloaded from iCloud, but nothing gets saved.

The files stay in your stream, but they're never there. There could be more than one reason for this:

- You have no (or a slow) internet connection
- Your iCloud storage is full
- The footage that was being downloaded now can't be located

More of the media we use for projects comes from iCloud libraries, especially the iCloud Photo Library. This means that the problem is more likely to happen on mobile devices. The Photos app on an Apple mobile device stores any video or screenshots that are taken. For many users, this app backs up to iCloud. It's also more likely to be a pain on the iOS and iPadOS apps because iMovie doesn't make copies of video files as it does on Mac. It is important to keep the source media safe on the device. If you don't, problems like this never-ending import can happen.

Solution – tidy up your iCloud storage

The media is not saved on the device when it is in the iCloud Photos Library. That's why you have to download it to your device before you can use it in iMovie. **What you can do to fix the issue is:**

- Make sure your internet link is strong
- Getting rid of files you don't need from your iCloud storage
- Make sure you haven't deleted the footage you need for your project by checking the Recently Deleted folder in the Photos app.

If you have a fast internet link, getting things on your device shouldn't take more than a few minutes. It's possible that the download was stopped because of iCloud storage limits if the files are still stuck. If you don't pay for more iCloud storage, Apple devices will happily tell you that your storage is full, even if it's not quite full.

Here's a quick way to free up room in your iCloud storage if you get a storage warning:

1. Check to see what movies, songs, and voice memos you can delete from your iCloud storage without risk, and then do it. By "safely," I mean that you should never delete files that are connected to your video.
2. Find the files you want to delete forever in the Recently Deleted folder for each app, like Photos or Voice Memos. Make sure you don't need them again before deleting them for good. Before that's done, you won't be able to save any room.
3. In the Settings app, go to the iCloud area. Look at the apps that are linked to iCloud and remove them if you don't want them to sync. My best things to uncheck? News and stocks.
4. If you still need to make room, copy all of your largest iCloud files to the Files app on your iPhone or iPad or the Finder on your Mac. These could be movies in your Photos library. After that, get rid of the files from iCloud. That way, your files will be safe and a lot of space will be cleared up.

If you can't find the footage you wanted to use and it's not in the Recently Deleted folder, it's probably gone for good and can't be recovered. You will have to record something new then, which is sad. There's also a bigger issue at play. When you download something through iCloud, it doesn't always work well with iMovie. It comes up a lot in the iMovie boards, and it doesn't look like it's being fixed in new versions of iMovie. So, the best way to escape this problem is to not store big files like your clips (recorded footage before editing) in iCloud.

Long-term solution – remove project media from iCloud libraries

You don't have to take dangerous steps to fix a project that stopped working in the middle of editing because the iCloud download problem stops you from adding media to the timeline in the first place. We can keep the recording files on the device so that the iCloud problem doesn't happen again by starting over.

On phones and tablets:

1. Open the Photos app.
2. Look for the clip and pick it.
3. Click on the Share button.
4. Press "**Save**" and then "**File**."
5. Give the file a name that you can remember and open the Files app on your iPhone or iPad. Press "**Save**."
6. Get out of the menu and delete the video from Photos.

If you used the built-in Photos library in iMovie's left-hand Libraries pane, you might have had trouble with iCloud downloads on a Mac. **On a Mac, here's how to stop your media from being synced with iCloud:**

1. Find the media you want to use in your video in the Photos app.
2. Click on each video you want to use. Each one will have a checkmark next to it, which means it has been chosen.

3. Drag all of these videos out of the Photos app. This makes copies of the movies that you can then add to Finder.
4. Put the media into a folder that will be used for your video project.
5. Go back to the Photos app and get rid of the movies you copied.

It might be best to leave those videos in the **Recently Deleted** folder while you edit since we're not worried about iCloud storage space in this case. Since you're not using iCloud, downloading won't go wrong, and the source movies will still be around in case something goes wrong. Don't forget that it's best to keep copies. It's also a good idea to leave at least 10% of your available space empty. When a device's storage is more than 90% full, apps run more slowly and strange things start to happen. That should fix the problem with getting it from iCloud. Now that the media is properly loaded into iMovie, let's talk about some issues that might arise while you're editing the clips.

Problem – audio and video drift out of sync

You will need to sync the two in the timeline if you took video and audio separately, perhaps using a different camera and microphone.
1. Look for a clear visual cue in your video for a short, sharp sound, like the sound of drums or a clap.
2. Use an M to mark that spot in the video. Then, find the beginning of the sound in the audio track, pick it, and mark that spot too.
3. Move the audio tags so that they are both in the same spot. If you turn on Snapping (N), the marks will be drawn together when they are close.

But here's the problem: the video and audio may have been exactly in time at the beginning of the video, but by the end, they may have moved so that the audio is ahead of the video, or the other way around. What's going on there? If you record audio and video at different times, the rates at which they are taken might not match up. It's almost certain to happen, and the longer the video, the clearer it is. The automatic tools in NLEs like Final Cut Pro can fix this, and iMovie, which is meant to be an NLE that "just works," should also have them. However, you have to change the speed of the video in iMovie to make this fix.

Solution – change the speed of the audio clip

One of the audio or video streams needs to be sped up or slowed down to match the other when they start to drift apart during the video. It would be better to change the audio because it is smaller, which makes it faster and easier to make changes. **So, here's how to fix the shifting issue and make sure the audio and video are in sync with each other:**
1. Make sure that the audio and video are in sync at a point near the beginning of the video.
2. Near the end of the video, find a sound that goes with a clear visual cue. Mark the visual cue with an M.
3. Mark the spot on the audio file where the sound starts. At the beginning of the project, you synced the video and audio. By the end, the marks might be in a different place.
4. Press Command Key + R while the audio is playing to launch the Speed Editor.

5. Fifth, move the circle at the end of the audio clip so that the two marks line up. If you turn on snapping (N), the marks will join together when they get close.
6. Press the Shift Key and Z to zoom out of the timeline. Then, make sure that both sets of two marks at the sync points are still lined up.

There is no need to be concerned about the audience's experience being negatively impacted by the change in audio speed. A speed change of no more than 1% to 2% can fix the audio drift that happens about once every 20 minutes in a video. To help smooth over the change, you can always check the box next to Preserve Pitch in the Speed toolbar choice. There you have it: a way to fix audio drift. iMovie needs to be closed and then opened again if you're having other issues with clips while editing, especially if they're not doing what these steps say they should. Most of the problems should be fixed now. But even if your clips are working fine, you may still run into problems as you get deeper into a more complicated edit.

Problem – editing on iMovie is slow or choppy

It's not always clear what causes iMovie to be slow when editing and stuttering is one of them. If restarting iMovie doesn't work, you should restart your Mac.

But be careful when you do this:

- Wait for any iMovie jobs that are running to finish (look at the white circle in the upper right corner of the iMovie window).
- Press the Command Key and Q to close iMovie and check that your work was saved.
- Restart your Mac.
- Open iMovie again. Open only the iMovie Libraries you need for the project if you have more than one. This will make iMovie work better.

If restarting iMovie doesn't help, it's time to figure out what's wrong. The first thing you should do to figure out what's wrong is to ask yourself if you're working on a very hard job. **Your Mac may be having trouble rendering all the clips in the timeline if:**
- The project settings are set to 4K and/or a high frame rate
- There are a lot of uncompressed effects in the project, such as titles, green/blue screens, and PiP keyframing.
- The clip speeds change a lot, and the more they speed up, the more intense this is.
- The project is long (over 20 minutes).

There aren't many of these that we want to change. If the timeline is in high resolution or has a lot of effects, and you have good reasons for doing this, you shouldn't have to give up parts of the project to work on it. The following options, from simplest to most extreme, are all possible. Give them a try, in this order.

Solution 1 – change the project settings

The project settings should be fixed if you're working in a timeline with a higher resolution and/or frame rate than the one you want to export. **This will make things easier for both you and iMovie. To:**

- Press Command Key + N to make a new project, and then add the right project type file to the timeline.
- Press 2 to return to the Projects screen, then click twice on the first project.
- Press **Command Key + A and Command Key + C** to make a copy of the whole timeline of your first project.
- Add the clips to the new project by pressing the Command Key and V after the project style clip.
- Get rid of the project format clip and begin editing again.

There should be less trouble with editing now that a 1080p project has only a quarter as many pixels to deal with as a 4K project. Things may still be moving more slowly because of the effects of the project if they aren't getting better.

Solution 2 – compound your effects

iMovie effects put a lot of stress on your Mac's graphics, but they still need to be created like any other clip. Because of this, going through a part with a lot of effects or that is sped up a lot is likely to slow things down because your Mac is having trouble keeping up with everything at the same time. You don't have to do this if iMovie doesn't see the effects as effects, or if the effects are just regular clips. It's the same process to make a single clip from a PiP, overlay, green screen, animation title, and other things. **You only need to export the clips and combine them into a single effect that you can then import again:**

1. Make a new project and copy the clips that are part of your effect.
2. Look at the result, make changes, and try again. When you're happy with it, go to **File | Share | File.**
3. When you export the effect, make sure that you choose **Best (ProRes)** from the Quality drop-down box. This is especially important if you plan to edit the clip again.
4. Once the export is done, add the combined effect to your original project. This will replace the different clips that made up the effect before.

Combining effects makes your Mac's graphics work less hard, and if you save the project where you put the effect, you can change the original effect whenever you need to. But if the first job is still taking too long, you may need to divide it into more manageable pieces.

Solution 3 – split the project into multiple timelines

If your project is longer than 20 minutes, iMovie might move a lot more slowly. This result is caused by the fact that more and more clips need to be produced. It might help to find breaks in your video where you can split it into different pieces if the work on the timeline is too stuttery to keep going. **Here are some rules for how to divide the work:**

- For **narrative**, split at the end of a thought, line, or (better yet) scene.
- For **visuals**: Split when going from full-frame color to black, white, or any other color
- For **audio**: Split when all the sound has gone away.

Why do we have to think so hard about how to divide the project? For this method, QuickTime Player is used to put back together the different parts of your project because saving all of your projects from a single timeline would take too long. It's much faster to combine movies in QuickTime Player than to process and export from an NLE. But since we're using QuickTime Player, we need to separate our timelines since we can't blend the music and video later. Stay away from audio-filled areas so that the sound doesn't jump around. Also, finishing each project on a block-color screen makes it easy to keep the visual flow. If you keep each project to a scene of your video instead of splitting them up by project time alone, there's a good reason given for why you might edit one project differently than the next. It's never a good idea to split up a project like this, but these tips will help us lessen the effect and still make the video we want. There shouldn't be more than a couple of seconds of silence between projects. An accurate 0.5-second fade to a color background at the end of one project could help you do this. Then you would start the next project with the opposite: 0.5 seconds of background color that fades into the first scene of the next project. Once you're satisfied with a project, save it as usual, choosing the best grade that fits (since you have more than one project).

Once you've done this for all of your video's parts, you can use QuickTime Player to put the whole thing together:

- Open the export file for the first part in QuickTime Player.
- To get to Clips mode, press the Command Key + E.
- Drag the exported file from the second part over the QuickTime Player window and drop it where it should go after the first part.
- Do this for every part of the video. When you're done with the last part of the export, hit "**Done**" in the QuickTime Player window.
- Save the whole project as one video by clicking **File | Export**.

To keep iMovie from slowing down, you can split the project as many times as you need to. Just keep in mind that each time, the video will not move as easily and will look less connected. You should make as few different parts as iMovie will still let you. What's going on? Your Mac may be having trouble because it has less than 10% of its storage room left. iMovie may also be a big reason for this.

Problem – iMovie constantly fills hard drive space

Your hard drive can get full while editing in iMovie, even if you don't add any new clips. You can see what's using up room by going to **Apple Menu | About This Mac | Storage | Manage**. The iMovie Library is taking up almost as much space as the movies you put there.

If you remember, iMovie for macOS makes a copy of each video file you add. When you think about how much space your project will need, you need to double it. For example, a 20 GB movie file will take up to 40 GB on your Mac once you start editing it. This isn't what's taking up space on your Mac, though. Making render files is what it does. If you have render files, it's easier to play your timeline without stops and starts. During this processing process, iMovie is exporting your movie while you change it. You can render as you go with some other NLEs, but if you don't, the export time will be much longer. The trouble is that the iMovie Library keeps getting bigger in the background because render files are being made automatically.

Solution – delete render files

The good news is that you can easily get rid of the render files that have been made if your iMovie Library gets too big:

1. Go to **iMovie | iMovie Preferences** (*Command Key + ,*).
2. To delete the files, click the "**Delete**" button next to them.
3. Leave iMovie open for a few minutes while it makes the bare minimum of image files that you need to edit easily.

It's that easy. When you delete render files, you don't get rid of any of the media you've uploaded or any clips on any timeline. The only bad thing about this is that exports will take a lot longer. Due to this, if you have enough room and are about to export a project, it's best to wait to delete render files until after the export.

Important: Don't forget step 3. If you try to change right after deleting render files, the process will be very slow and jumpy. Getting rid of render files is like taking out the junk on a drive. If you press the "**Delete**" button, your computer will automatically fix any big problems that are making it take longer to use. This is something you don't have to do all the time. The broken-up hard drive, or image files in iMovie's case, isn't the bad guy to begin with. For that reason, don't keep trying to get rid of render files. They are there to make updating easier.

So far, the problem/solution notes should have covered most of the strange issues that could come up while you're working in iMovie. Now we'll talk about problems you might have when shipping.

Problem – iMovie export has failed

Errors in exporting are pretty scary. They do not let your video happen, so you cannot ignore them. They're also hard to understand, but there is a way to get them. iMovie makes export mistakes when it can't find the footage that makes up clips in the timeline or when the footage is damaged. This issue usually doesn't show up until the export, so moving your movie and adjusting it again might not be a good idea. If an iMovie export fails, a sign will show up telling you that the export failed. Click on this because it has the information you need to figure out what's wrong. The important part of the letter is the number that comes at the end, after everything else.

Solution 1 – find and delete the problem frame

This message tells you the number of the first frame where iMovie had a problem. The trouble frame is probably close to the beginning if your export failed quickly. It's likely close to the end if it failed right before the progress circle in the upper right corner of the iMovie window closed. The mistake message from iMovie tells us the exact frame number, but that number is often in the thousands. How do we figure that out? We only need to do the following math:

Problem frame number/frame rate of project

Let's say the mistake happened at frame 10,085, and the project is running at 60 frames per second:

1. Split the number of frames by the number of frames per second (10,085/60 = 168.0833).
2. For now, don't worry about what comes after the decimal point. The whole number tells you how many seconds are left in your project.
   - The 168th second, or 2 minutes and 48 seconds into the project, is where our trouble frame is.
3. Press the play button on that second of the video. We're looking for a dropped frame, which can be seen in the Viewer by a black screen for one frame. Put the playhead on the dropped frame if you can see it, and go to step 7.
4. We can figure out the exact frame to cut out if the trouble can't be seen. Multiply the number that's left over by the project's frame rate (0.0833*60 = 4.988).
5. Round the number to the next whole number, whether it's up or down. The closest whole number in this case is 5, so that's how many frames are in a second. So, the issue will be at timecode 02:48:05, which is the 5th frame of the 168th second of the movie.
6. Use the arrow keys to get to the fifth picture of the second.
7. Cut the trouble frame down to size. To do this, press Command Key + B to split the project at the playhead point and then press, to trim back one frame:
   - These changes won't affect how you watch the movie, but they should let you export it.
8. Does the export process all over again? If there's a new mistake, this one should help with the job later on. If you get a new error, do these steps again. If you still get an error, jump to the next option.

This is another iMovie problem that shows why you should convert your footage first: it can help you avoid dropped frames and has other benefits too, like making the file smaller and making sure it works with other programs. In this case, though, trouble frames may keep showing up even after you've cut them out twice. Then you need to know how to make the mistake. It's time to trick the export process.

Solution 2 – screen-record the project

iMovie will sometimes force you to give up on sharing your project no matter how hard you try. You'll have to find a different way to make a video from your history then. This problem is more likely to happen if the project takes longer and is more complicated. It happens in other NLEs too. For example, the 40-minute or so YouTube video Cost of Concordia, which was edited in the paid NLE Adobe Premiere Pro, had a lot of problems with exporting. It had to be screen-recorded several times, put back together, and posted. We also need to record the sound from the timeline to screen-record a project. Macs have built-in screen recordings, but they don't have a built-in way to record sound. Here's where Blackhole 2ch comes in. It's a virtual audio driver that, once set up, lets you pick your Mac as a sound source.

Once it's loaded, follow these steps to get it to work for screen recording a project:

1. Go to **Apple Menu | System Settings | Sound**:
If you're using macOS 12 (Monterey) or previous, **System Settings** will be listed as **System Preferences.**
2. In the **Output** tab, select **Blackhole 2ch**:
If the Blackhole gadget isn't shown, the update doesn't go as planned, and you'll have to do it again.
Now that the computer's sound is sending to our sound recorder, we can set up the screen recording:
- To get to the macOS Screenshot and Recording Options screen, press the **Command Key, the Shift Key**, and **5**.
- Click the option that says "Record Whole Screen."
- Make sure Microphone is set to BlackHole 2ch in the Options drop-down menu:

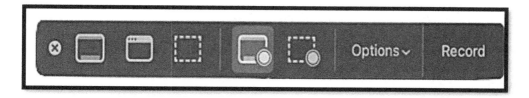

- To close the menu bar, press the Esc key.
- Startup iMovie and find the project you want to record the screen for.
- Click anywhere on the timeline to set the playhead to 0:00.
- Press the **Command Key + Shift Key + 5** to bring up the recording options bar again. THEN click **Record**.
- After a few seconds, press the Shift Key, the Command Key, and the F key to play the project in full-screen mode.
- Wait a couple of seconds more after the video is over. Once more, press the **Command Key + Shift Key + 5** and then click the button in the middle to stop writing.

The recording will likely be saved to the desktop, which is where the option was chosen in the screenshot and recording options box. Now, all that's left to do is clean up the recording:

- First, double-click on the file to play it in QuickTime Player.
- To get into Trim mode, press the Command Key + T.
- Cut out the clips that come before and after the video so that the finished video doesn't have any blank spots. Press Trim.
- Click on File and then Export As. If your Mac's screen resolution is high enough, QuickTime Player might let you export in 4K. However, you should only export in the resolution that iMovie set the project to.

After that, you should have a video that you can either share or post. You should only record your screen for a project as a last option, though. Your computer won't look smooth during the recording if it doesn't have enough power. Frames will be dropped as your Mac tries to play the project and record the screen at the same time. All of this can make the video pointless to watch in the end. To get around this, catch small chunks of the video on your screen at a time and then put them back together. But, as we explained in Solution 3, fixing the gaps between records takes a long time and is hard to do when there are sound and complicated images to match up. So, the safest thing to do is to keep your screen recording as a copy of the video and keep trying to export the original, if you can handle it. A file that has been saved and made is always the best result. Finally, let's look at what you should do if you run into a problem that isn't on this list.

What if my editing issue isn't listed here?

There are a lot of problems that happen when editing because of how iMovie and other Apple apps are made. That's not an excuse, but it does mean that the problem isn't with the method or the way things are done; it just needs a different approach.

General solutions for general problems

Here are some steps you can try to see if they help if you are having trouble with iMovie that we haven't already mentioned a way to fix. **You may have to go through the first few steps several times when editing:**

- Press 2 to return to the Projects screen, then double-click to return to your project:
  - You could also click on the timeline. It might sound strange, but depending on where your mouse is, changing can be hard because it gets stuck in the Media Browser.
- Close iMovie and open it again.
- Make sure that the iMovie Preferences (Command Key +,) are set to the defaults:

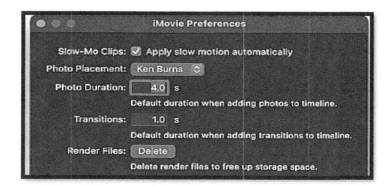

- Restart your Mac.
- Make a new timeline and copy your project files into it.
- If there is an update for macOS, download and install a minor update (like version 12.4 to 12.5) or a patch update (like 12.6.1 to 12.6.2).
- Look up the issue online and post a question in help groups if you can't find an answer:
  - You can find an iMovie community group on the Apple website at *https://discussions.apple.com/community/ilife/imovie*. On Reddit, there is a community called **r/iMovie** at *https://www.reddit.com/r/iMovie*. At the time this was written, both were active support groups.

It might be time for some bigger changes if the internet's combined knowledge can't help. You should be careful with these, though, and be ready. Get rid of any projects that aren't finished, **then back up all of your clips and other project media, and finally, save your iMovie Library to an external drive or the cloud:**

- Delete the iMovie app first, and then get it again from the Mac App Store. Launchpad should be on the Dock, but if it's not, it will be in the Applications folder. Right-click on the iMovie icon to do this. To get rid of the app, click the "x" icon:

Lastly, you should make a full copy of your Mac on an external drive before you do these steps. If these changes make it harder to use your Mac in general, you'll want to go back to the way things were before. You can't make these changes again without a backup. **Before you try any of these, make sure you know how to use System Settings to make a backup with macOS's Time Machine:**

- If there is a big update for macOS, like macOS Monterey to Ventura, download and run it.
- Delete and reinstall macOS itself, to start afresh.

If you want to get rid of everything on your hard drive, reinstalling macOS is the best way to fix any problem with iMovie. This includes apps, settings, preferences, and more. Because the issue might be with system-level files that you should never change, this method can help you fix issues that you couldn't before. Just keep in mind that buying a new Mac is rarely the answer to any problem. It's up to Apple to make sure that its apps work properly on its computers. It's their job to try to help you find a solution, guarantee or not if a fresh copy of macOS doesn't fix the problem and your Mac isn't a very old one.

Tips for Optimizing Performance and Stability

1. **Update iMovie**: Ensure you have the latest version of iMovie installed. Updates often include bug fixes and performance improvements.
2. **Check System Requirements**: Make sure your Mac meets the system requirements for running iMovie. Running it on a compatible system will ensure smoother performance.
3. **Close Background Apps**: Close any unnecessary applications running in the background to free up system resources for iMovie.
4. **Use Optimized Media**: iMovie allows you to optimize your media for smoother editing. When importing media choose the option to optimize for better performance. This converts your media to a format that is easier for iMovie to work with.
5. **Adjust Playback Quality**: In the iMovie preferences, you can adjust the playback quality. Lowering the playback quality can improve performance, especially on older or less powerful Macs.
6. **Reduce Project Size**: Large projects with many clips, effects, and transitions can slow down iMovie. Consider splitting your project into smaller sections or removing unnecessary elements to reduce the project size.
7. **Close Other Projects**: If you have multiple iMovie projects open, close the ones you're not actively working on to conserve system resources.
8. **Clear Cache**: iMovie may accumulate cache files over time, which can affect performance. Periodically clear the cache by going to iMovie > Preferences > Cache and clicking on the "Delete Cache Files" button.
9. **Use External Storage**: If your Mac's internal storage is running low, consider storing your iMovie library and media files on an external drive. This can free up space and improve performance.
10. **Restart iMovie/Mac**: Sometimes, simply restarting iMovie or your Mac can resolve performance issues caused by temporary glitches or memory leaks.
11. **Check for Updates**: Ensure that all plugins or third-party software you're using with iMovie are up to date. Outdated plugins can cause stability issues.
12. **Disable Background Rendering**: If you're experiencing stability issues during editing, try disabling background rendering in iMovie preferences. This can prevent iMovie from using excessive system resources while you're working.

Frequently Asked Questions about iMovie

1. **What is iMovie?**
   - iMovie is a video editing software application developed by Apple Inc. It allows users to edit and create videos on macOS and iOS devices.

2. **Is iMovie free?**
   - Yes, iMovie is free for macOS and iOS users. It comes pre-installed on most Mac computers and can be downloaded for free from the App Store on iOS devices.

3. **Can I use iMovie on Windows?**
   - No, iMovie is exclusive to macOS and iOS devices. There is no official version of iMovie for Windows.

4. **What file formats does iMovie support?**
   - iMovie supports a wide range of video and audio file formats, including MP4, MOV, AVI, M4V, MPEG-2, and more. It also supports various image formats such as JPEG, PNG, TIFF, etc.

5. **Can I add music to my iMovie project?**
   - Yes, iMovie allows you to add music to your projects. You can import music from your iTunes library or other sources and place it in your timeline to accompany your video.

6. **How do I export my iMovie project?**
   - To export your iMovie project, go to the File menu and select "Share" > "File." Choose the desired resolution and quality settings, and then click "Next" to specify the file name and destination. Finally, click "Save" to export your project.

7. **Can I add text and titles to my iMovie project?**
   - Yes, iMovie provides various text and title options that you can use to add captions, credits, and other text elements to your videos.

8. **How do I add effects and transitions in iMovie?**
   - To add effects and transitions, simply drag and drop them onto your clips in the timeline. iMovie offers a variety of built-in effects and transitions that you can use to enhance your videos.

9. **Is there a limit to the length of my iMovie project?**
   - iMovie does not impose a strict limit on the length of your projects. However, longer projects may require more storage space and processing power.

10. **Can I use iMovie to edit 4K videos?**
    - Yes, iMovie supports editing and exporting 4K videos on compatible Mac computers and iOS devices. However, editing 4K footage may require more system resources and processing power.

11. **Can I use iMovie to create trailers?**
    - Yes, iMovie offers a feature called "Trailers" which allows you to create professional-looking movie trailers easily. You can choose from various templates, add your footage and titles, and customize the trailer to your liking.

12. **Does iMovie support green screen (chroma key) effects?**
    - Yes, iMovie includes a green screen (chroma key) effect that allows you to replace the background of a video clip with another image or video. This feature is useful for creating special effects and compositing scenes.

13. **How do I import videos into iMovie?**
    - You can import videos into iMovie by clicking on the "Import Media" button in the toolbar or by dragging and dropping video files directly into the iMovie library. From there, you can drag the imported clips into your project timeline to begin editing.

14. **Can I use iMovie to edit videos recorded on my iPhone or iPad?**
    - Yes, iMovie seamlessly integrates with the Camera app on iOS devices, allowing you to easily edit videos recorded on your iPhone or iPad directly in iMovie. You can transfer videos to your Mac for further editing if needed.

15. **Does iMovie support multi-camera editing?**
    - Yes, iMovie offers multi-camera editing capabilities, allowing you to synchronize and switch between multiple camera angles in your project. This feature is useful for editing videos of live events or interviews captured from multiple cameras.

16. **Is there a way to speed up or slow down video clips in iMovie?**
    - Yes, iMovie allows you to adjust the speed of video clips by applying the "Speed" effect. You can speed up or slow down clips to create dramatic or comedic effects, or to fit the timing of your project.

17. **Can I share my iMovie projects directly with social media platforms?**
    - Yes, iMovie offers built-in sharing options that allow you to export and upload your projects directly to popular social media platforms such as YouTube, Facebook, and Vimeo. You can also share projects via email or Messages.

18. **Does iMovie offer tutorials or help resources for beginners?**
    - Yes, iMovie provides built-in tutorials and help resources to assist beginners in learning how to use the software. You can access these tutorials from the Help menu within iMovie or visit the Apple Support website for more in-depth guides and troubleshooting tips.

19. **Can I add voice overs or narration to my iMovie project?**
    - Yes, iMovie allows you to easily record and add voice overs or narration to your video projects. You can use the built-in microphone on your Mac or iOS device to record audio directly into iMovie and then place it on the timeline alongside your video clips.

20. **Is there a way to stabilize shaky footage in iMovie?**
    - Yes, iMovie includes a feature called "Stabilization" that can help reduce the shakiness of handheld or unstable footage. You can apply this effect to your video clips to smooth out camera movements and improve overall video quality.

CHAPTER 16

EXPLORING ADVANCED FEATURES AND THIRD-PARTY PLUGINS

Discovering Advanced Features in iMovie Pro

Creating Stunning Visual Effects

One great thing about iMovie is that it lets you add beautiful visual effects to your movies. You can turn a normal video into a movie creation with just a few taps. There are many effects in the app, such as slow motion, fast forward, and quick playback. To make your movies look different, you can also try out different effects and overlays. Import your video into the iMovie app, then tap on the clip you want to edit to add visual effects. Choose from a variety of options by clicking "Effects" from the menu. Before you add an effect, you can watch a clip of it to see how it changes the video. When you're happy with the result, click "Apply" and watch as the animations bring your video to life.

Advanced Audio Editing Techniques

iMovie has more advanced audio editing tools than just visual effects tools, so you can give your fans a fully immersive experience. iMovie can help you whether you want to improve the sound or add music in the background. Tap on the clip that has the audio you want to change in iMovie to edit it. Select "Audio" from that menu to see a list of options, including volume control, fade-in and fade-out effects, and even the ability to replace the audio with custom soundtracks from your iTunes library. You can make sure that your video, including the audio, is flawless by using these tools.

Utilizing Green Screen Effects

Have you ever thought about how professional directors make those amazing scenes where players look like they're in faraway places when they're actually in the studio? Green screen effects are the key, and iMovie makes it very easy to make your videos look like they were shot in Hollywood. Import your video and put it on the timeline in iMovie to use green screen effects. After that, tap on the clip and pick "**Green Screen**." After that, pick a picture or video to use as a background instead of the green screen. iMovie will find the green color and replace it with the background you choose. You can make the effect even better by changing things like the color and edge recognition. You can get to any place in the world with this tool without ever leaving your house.

Sharing Your Masterpiece

iMovie's share button lets you show off your video to the world once you're done changing it. Thank goodness iMovie has many sharing options that make it simple to share your work on social media sites or even export it for business use. The "Share" button is in the upper right corner of iMovie. Click it to send your video to someone else. Choose whether to share your video straight to social media sites like Instagram or YouTube, or export it as a file that you can email or share in another way. Also, before you share, you can change settings like size and quality to make sure that your video always looks its best.

Exploring Third-Party Plugins and Extensions for iMovie

If you have the most recent version of iMovie, the apps will not work. That was because plug-in software doesn't work with the latest versions of iMovie. iMovie works fine on both Mac and iOS, but you might still have problems if your video file is in an MKV, WMV, AVI, FLV, VOB, or other format. Additionally, if you use Windows, you should look for another effect to meet your needs for advanced video editing. There are a lot of iMovie apps out there, but which ones are the best depends on your needs. You can use any of the apps' special features while making videos because they are all fully compatible with iMovie.

Below are a few important details about the top five tools:
   1. **ASCII & ART**
This tool is very good and easy to use, so you will enjoy it. ASCII & ART can give you a great time making videos because it has a lot of cool artsy effects that don't cost too much. A lot of people love this tool because it can convert pictures and movies at the fastest speed.
   2. **Big & Bold**
Because of its easy-to-use and complicated design, this is one of the best iMovie apps out there. With its great features, users will have full control over both titles and text, and they can quickly change them by adding flexible motion-changing elements.
   3. **Crops & Zooms**
You will be able to enjoy simple zooming as well as a few advanced effects like circle, square, blocky, or ultra-smooth peephole with the Crop & Zoom app. Also, you can use special ramp effects on movies. The best thing about it is that you can combine so many effects or changes, like spin, shrink, stretch, flip, and more, to make something awesome. This set of changes can also be used for cartoons on the iMovie platform that use the camera shakes effect.
   4. **Gree Three slick**
Ten different files come with this plugin. Each one has hundreds of effects, transitions, and titles. You will save almost 40% of your total cost if you choose to use Gree Three Slick with iMovie. Thanks to its award-winning performance, this tool can help professionals make amazing video clips. Anyone can also use it to make cartoons that look like Hollywood movie series.
   5. **iBubble**
This app has thirteen different titles that you can use. It has speech bubbles, lines, and labels, thought bubbles, simple text, moving text, bright text effects, and more. The main reason for its

huge success is that it's easy to use and has advanced features that can help you make great videos with little work.

Plugin Installation and Integration

If you're ready to add iMovie apps and want to know how to get them on your device, the information below can help. There are a lot of people, who have trouble installing iMovie plugins, but you don't need to call an expert to do it; if you follow the right steps, you can do it in seconds.

     o   **Save Plugin files to the right folder**

A lot of people keep their plugins in the plugin folder that is made in the Applications: iMovie resource area. But that's not where you should normally keep your plugin files because they are hard to find and run when you need to. Experts suggest creating a special folder for plugins inside the Library of your system. All you have to do is go to your device's library folder and then to the iMovie folder. Here is where you need to make a folder called "plugins" where you can store all of your backup plugin software. These tools can only show effects on your video timeline if they are correctly put inside the iMovie folder. If they are not, they will not show up on time in your video editing platform.

     o   **Save Plugin files to a specific disc**

Experts say that you should make a special area on your hard drive for plug-ins so that you can quickly access everything when you need to in real-time. Go to the hard disc drive and then find your username. This is where you should put all of your plug-ins. You will find the Library folder inside this folder. It holds the iMovie software and all of its important files. You can easily find this place in iMovie: go inside and make a plug-in folder. This helps to show all transitions and effects continuously, without any lag in performance. One important thing to keep in mind is that if you put your plug-ins in the iMovie App bundle, it might be hard to get help from these tools in the future. No one can figure out what changes iMovie patches made to the plugin folder because they are hidden. When you try to use the updated plugins for real-time writing, you will just get an error message, so it is best to make a different folder for them and keep them safe for later use.

Tips for Expanding Your Editing Capabilities with External Tools

1. **Use External Video and Audio Editors**: While iMovie offers a range of editing features, you may find that certain tasks are better suited to specialized software. Consider using external video and audio editors for advanced editing tasks such as color grading, audio mixing, or special effects. Programs like Adobe Premiere Pro, DaVinci Resolve, or Audacity can complement iMovie by providing additional tools and flexibility.

2. **Utilize Graphic Design Software**: Enhance your iMovie projects by incorporating elements created in graphic design software such as Adobe Photoshop or Illustrator. You can create custom titles, lower thirds, or overlays to give your videos a professional look. Export these graphics with transparent backgrounds for seamless integration into iMovie.

3. **Explore Animation Tools**: Add dynamic animations to your videos by using animation software like Adobe After Effects or Blender. Create custom animations for titles, transitions, or visual effects, then import them into iMovie as video files. This approach allows you to add polished animations to your projects beyond what's possible with iMovie's built-in features.

4. **Access Stock Footage and Audio Libraries**: Expand your content library by sourcing stock footage and audio from external libraries. Websites like Shutterstock, Pond5, or Envato Elements offer a vast selection of high-quality media assets that you can use to enhance your iMovie projects. Import these assets into iMovie to add professional polish and variety to your videos.

5. **Incorporate Plug-ins and Effects Packs**: Explore third-party plug-ins and effects packs designed specifically for iMovie. These add-ons can extend iMovie's functionality by providing additional transitions, effects, and editing tools. Look for reputable developers and read user reviews to find plug-ins that suit your editing style and needs.

6. **Utilize Cloud Storage and Collaboration Tools**: Take advantage of cloud storage services like Google Drive, Dropbox, or iCloud to store and share your iMovie projects across devices. This allows you to seamlessly collaborate with team members or access your projects from anywhere with an internet connection. Additionally, cloud storage ensures that your project files are safely backed up and accessible whenever you need them.

7. **Learn Keyboard Shortcuts and Workflow Enhancements**: External tools aren't just limited to software applications. Invest time in learning keyboard shortcuts and workflow enhancements that can streamline your editing process in iMovie. Tools like BetterTouchTool or Keyboard Maestro allow you to customize keyboard shortcuts and automate repetitive tasks, saving you time and effort during editing.

External Tool Selection Criteria

Selecting the right external tools to complement your iMovie editing workflow is crucial for maximizing efficiency and achieving professional-quality results. **Here are some key criteria to consider when choosing external tools:**

1. **Compatibility**: Ensure that the external tool you choose is compatible with iMovie and your operating system. Check for compatibility requirements, such as supported file formats, system specifications, and integration options with iMovie.

2. **Features and Functionality**: Evaluate the features and functionality offered by the external tool. Consider whether it provides the specific capabilities you need to enhance your iMovie projects, such as advanced editing tools, effects, transitions, audio processing, or collaboration features.

3. **Ease of Use**: Opt for external tools that are user-friendly and intuitive, especially if you're new to video editing or working with iMovie. Look for tools with well-designed interfaces, clear documentation, and tutorials to help you get started quickly and easily.

4. **Performance and Stability**: Choose tools that offer reliable performance and stability to ensure a smooth editing experience. Check user reviews, performance benchmarks, and technical specifications to assess the tool's stability, responsiveness, and compatibility with your hardware setup.

5. **Cost and Value**: Consider the cost of the external tool relative to its features, functionality, and the value it provides to your editing workflow. Evaluate whether the price aligns with your budget and the benefits you expect to gain from using the tool.

6. **Support and Updates**: Look for tools that offer robust customer support and regular software updates. Consider the availability of technical support channels, such as documentation, online forums, email support, or live chat, to help you troubleshoot issues and get assistance when needed.

7. **Integration and Workflow**: Choose tools that seamlessly integrate with iMovie and complement your existing editing workflow. Look for integration options such as import/export compatibility, plugin support, file sharing, or cloud storage integration to streamline your editing process and enhance collaboration with team members.

8. **Reputation and Reviews**: Research the reputation of the external tool and read user reviews to gauge its reliability, performance, and user satisfaction. Look for testimonials, case studies, or recommendations from trusted sources to ensure that the tool meets your expectations and delivers the results you're looking for.

Workflow Integration Strategies

To successfully add additional tools to your iMovie process, you need to carefully plan and carry out your actions. You can make the most of iMovie and speed up the editing process by carefully thinking about your routine and choosing tools that work well with it. Before you start, you should figure out which parts of your iMovie process could use extra help. To choose the right tools for your workflow, you need to know what you want to achieve, whether it's adding more advanced editing features, making music processing better, or making it easier for team members to work together. When picking outside tools, they must work with iMovie. Look for tools that work with iMovie's file types and connection choices so that you can easily move project assets from iMovie to other programs. When looking at possible integration tools, think about things like how easy they are to use, what features they support, and how they can be integrated. Setting up clear rules for managing files is important for making it easy for iMovie and other programs to work together. Set up rules for file names, folder layouts, and how to organize files so that your project assets stay in order and are easy to find across all tools. This will help keep things clear and make sure that everyone on the team can work together effectively.

You can move project files between iMovie and other programs by importing and exporting them in iMovie. You can export video clips, audio files, or project plans from iMovie to other programs so that they can be changed further. After editing, you can bring the assets back into iMovie to finish putting them together. This process keeps things going and lets you use the best features of both iMovie and other programs. Check out plugins, addons, and add-ons that make iMovie more useful and let you connect it to other programs. To improve your editing process, look for apps that offer advanced editing tools, effects, transitions, or audio processing options. Adding these tools to your iMovie routine can help you be more creative and make edits go more quickly. Use cloud files, project management tools, or communication platforms to make it easier for team members to work together. Share project files, comments, and changes with your team in real-time. This makes it easy to talk to each other and work together while writing. You can make sure that everyone is working toward the same goal by making it easier for people to work together.

Automate jobs that you do over and over again and speed up your work with automation tools or scripts. To save time and effort while writing, you can automate chores like batch processing, file transfers, and metadata tagging. You can spend more time and energy on more creative parts of editing if you automate chores that you do over and over again. Stay adaptable and open to changes in how you work and the technology you use. Check your workflow integration strategies, tools, and processes regularly to find ways to make them better and increase their efficiency over time. You can make sure that your iMovie process stays quick and useful for editing by learning and changing things all the time. In conclusion, adding outside tools to your iMovie process needs careful thought and calculated execution. You can make iMovie more useful and speed up the editing process by figuring out your workflow needs, choosing tools that work well together, setting clear rules for managing files, and using plugins and extensions. To improve speed and make sure that your iMovie process stays useful over time, you should also make it easier for people to work together, automate jobs that you do over and over, and stay open to change.

Tips, tricks, and hacks for iMovie

1. Using Titles for Special Effects
Many names in iMovie can be used in unusual ways to make unique effects. To blur your movie, you can use the "Pull Focus" title. Just put the title over the clip you want to blur and get rid of the usual text. The video will now be blurred. You can also try different titles like **"Boogie Lights," "Pixie Dust,"** and **"Lens Flare"** to give certain parts of your video their unique drop-in effects.

2. Adding Color Tint to Videos
You can add a colored tint to your video by putting a background on top of the clip in iMovie. You can pick a background from a bunch of uniform colors or use an image editing app to make your picture. By changing how opaque the background is, you can add a soft or strong color tint to your movie. You can use this method to improve the mood or environment of your movie.

3. Using Backgrounds and Cutaways
You can be artistic with backgrounds and cutaways to make your movies more interesting to look at. iMovie has a lot of background designs that are already made and can be quickly added to your video and stretched to fit. You can make a fence around your video by putting a cutout on top of a background. This method works great when you want to draw attention to a certain part of your video or make a frame that looks good.

4. Taking Inspiration from Trailers
There are a lot of cool titles, backgrounds, and songs in iMovie that are made just for trailers. You won't be able to use these tools when working on a normal job. You can make a new document, though, and pick the "Trailer" choice instead. This will let you check out a bunch of cool backgrounds and names. After that, you can turn the clip into a full movie and use parts of it in your work.

5. Creative Transitions between Clips

There aren't many changes in iMovie, but you can be artistic by using them in different ways. For instance, you can add a black background and use transitions to make the clips run into each other smoothly. When you mix transitions with black backgrounds, you can get cool visual effects and make the change between scenes easier. This method makes your movies look more professional.

6. Adding Visual Effects with Transitions

You can also use transitions to make quick visual effects within the same clip. You can add a cross blur, cross zoom, or ripple effect by cutting the clip in half and putting the transition where you want it. You can use this method to make quick flashes or draw attention to certain parts of your video. Try out various changes and lengths of time to discover the best graphic effects for your video.

7. Using Emojis as Visual Elements

You can use images in the names of your videos to quickly add a visual feature without making a separate picture. For this method, the central title choice works best. You can choose an emoji figure, change its size and place it in the title. This adds a simple but useful visual feature to your movie like thumbs up to draw attention to a good moment.

8. Creating a Shaky Video Effect

You can make your steady footage look like it was taken with a small camera by putting your main clip, on top of a black background as a picture-in-picture effect. It is possible to make a shaky video effect by stretching the picture beyond the video's edges and adding keyframes to move it around at regular times. This method gives your video a more real and lively feel.

Conclusion

Apple's iMovie is a video editing program that is both flexible and user-friendly. It provides a wide variety of tools that are appropriate for users of all skill levels, from novices to experts. With its user-friendly interface, a wide library of effects, transitions, and titles, and seamless connection with other Apple products, iMovie makes it possible for artists to bring their ideas to life in a straightforward manner. You will be able to maximize performance, unlock creativity, and go on a voyage of narrative that will fascinate and inspire audiences if you follow the advice and make use of the tools that are offered in this book. Whether you are creating a personal video blog, a professional presentation, or a cinematic masterpiece, iMovie is there for you as a trustworthy friend. It gives you the ability to turn raw material into polished creations that create an impact that lasts. Therefore, immerse yourself in the world of iMovie, investigate its potential, and let your imagination run wild to create films that resonate with people all over the world and connect with these viewers. Enjoy your editing!

INDEX

B

N

O

P

Q

U

Made in the USA
Las Vegas, NV
31 May 2024

90495286R00125